D1360691

# GRISWOLD v. CONNECTICUT

# Griswold v. Connecticut

## CONTRACEPTION AND THE RIGHT OF PRIVACY

by
Susan C. Wawrose

Historic Supreme Court Cases
FRANKLIN WATTS
A Division of Grolier Publishing
New York London Hong Kong Sydney
Danbury, Connecticut

Photographs copyright ©: AP/Wide World Photos: pp. 8, 11, 98, 116, 120, 123; UPI/Bettmann: pp. 13, 29 (both), 32, 35, 36, 66, 89, 107, 109, 128; The Bettmann Archive: pp. 22, 23, 105 top left; The Library of Congress: p. 18; Planned Parenthood of New York: p. 25; Planned Parenthood of Connecticut: pp. 30, 84; Waterbury Hospital: p. 44; New Haven Colony Historical Society: p. 55; Collection of the Supreme Court of the United States/Harris & Ewing: pp. 78, 100, 105 bottom right; Virginia Blaisdell: p. 94.

Library of Congress Cataloging-in-Publication Data

Wawrose, Susan C.
    Griswold v. Connecticut: contraception and the right of privacy / Susan C. Wawrose
        p.  cm.— (Historic Supreme Court cases)
    Includes bibliographical references and index.
    Summary: Discusses the case which identified a constitutional right of privacy for married people to use contraception and points out the significance of the ruling.
    ISBN 0-531-11249-7
    1. Griswold, Estelle—Trials, litigation, etc.  2. Trials—Connecticut—New Haven.  3. Birth control—Law and legislation—Connecticut.  4. Privacy, Right of—Connecticut. [1. Griswold, Estelle—Trials, litigation, etc.  2. Trials.  3. Birth control.  4. Privacy, Right of.]  I. Title  II. Series.

KF224.G75W39  1996
342.746'0858—dc20
[347.4602858]                                                    95-46076  CIP  AC

# CONTENTS

# GRISWOLD v. CONNECTICUT

*Estelle Griswold, executive director of
the Planned Parenthood League in
Connecticut and named party in*
Griswold v. Connecticut

# Chapter 1

# THE BIRTH CONTROL CONTROVERSY IN CONNECTICUT

It was a sunny afternoon in early November 1961 when detectives John Blazi and Harold Berg interrupted Estelle Griswold at work. They were on a raid, looking for evidence that a long-standing Connecticut law was being violated. They found the proof they needed in Griswold's office on the second floor of a grand old mansion in New Haven, Connecticut.

Griswold met the detectives at the top of the stairs and told them right away that, indeed, she was breaking the law. (She may even have greeted John Blazi by name; a few years earlier she had presented him with a civic award.) Then she took the detectives on a tour of the "criminal" operation that she was running. It was a Planned Parenthood center—a birth control clinic—and operating such a center was strictly illegal.

Ms. Griswold, a stately woman in her early sixties, carefully pointed out the condoms and other contraceptives they dispensed at the clinic—evidence enough for an arrest to be made. As she showed them the center, Griswold told the detectives that she hoped the law would be enforced so that she could challenge its validity before the U.S. Supreme Court. She said she welcomed arrest but would refuse to hand over patient records. "It was one of the easiest types of investigations you could get involved in," Berg recalled some years later. "It wasn't one of those investigations where you had to dig out the information. . . . It was sort of 'Here it is; here we are; take us in.' "[1]

James Morris, the night manager of a nearby Avis Rent-A-Car agency, had informed the police. Morris, a forty-two-year-old Roman Catholic and the father of five, called the police to complain as soon as he heard what Estelle Griswold was up to. "[It's] like a house of prostitution," he charged.[2] Morris was persistent in pursuing an official response to Griswold's center. He contacted the Connecticut state police, the New Haven police, and the New Haven mayor. When Morris finally appeared in person in the office of Julius Maretz, the circuit court prosecutor, Maretz agreed to request a police investigation into the clinic.

Estelle Griswold's center was not a back-alley joint where unmarried girls paid a lot of money to avoid pregnancy. The clinic, clean and well run, was staffed by experienced doctors and nurses who provided contraception and family-planning advice to low-income married women. Patients were never charged more than fifteen dollars for visits, and services were much in demand. In the ten days the clinic was open, forty-two patients were seen and seventy-five more applied for appointments. When word of the police "raid" reached the patients who were in the clinic's examination rooms at the time,

*A one-man campaign against the birth
control movement, James Morris pickets in
front of the Planned Parenthood Center
of New Haven, Connecticut.*

one determined woman remarked, "We're going on a sit-down strike until we get what we came for."[3]

Detectives Blazi and Berg left empty-handed that day, but they would return. James Morris continued his tirade, declaring "every moment the clinic stays open another child is not born."[4] The local press kept asking, "Will the state uphold the law?" Prosecutor Maretz declined to comment.

One week later, on November 10, Judge J. Robert Lacey of the Sixth Circuit Court of Connecticut and Maretz issued arrest warrants for the clinic's executive director, Griswold, and medical director, Dr. Charles Lee Buxton. Griswold and Buxton appeared voluntarily in New Haven police court and pleaded not guilty. The charges? Violating Connecticut laws that made the use of contraceptives illegal and forbade citizens from assisting anyone in the commission of a crime. According to the arrest warrant, the defendants "did assist, abet, counsel, cause, and command certain married women to use any drug, medicinal article or instrument for the purpose of preventing conception." After posting bail of $100, Griswold and Buxton were released. No fingerprints or mug shots had been taken.

That same day, Planned Parenthood voluntarily closed the clinic. Morris must have been satisfied to see it close, but he vowed to remain vigilant. "It is against the natural law, which says marital relations are for procreation and not entertainment. . . . Every time they try to open a birth-control clinic, I will force its closing, as long as the law is on the books." Morris felt strongly that the clinic had done "an awful lot of damage." Still, the leaders of Planned Parenthood welcomed his attention. In the words of one official: "He fell right into our laps."[5]

*Estelle Griswold (right) and C. Lee Buxton (center)
are shown in police headquarters after their arrest
for dispensing contraceptives in 1961.*

### REASONS FOR THE STRUGGLE

Even though birth control was illegal in Connecticut, it was widely available. Many private doctors simply ignored the law and prescribed birth control for their patients. Drugstores filled the prescriptions and sold condoms under the counter. Those Connecticut citizens able to travel to neighboring states, such as New York and Rhode Island, also had access to a full range of contraceptives and family-planning services. Why, then, would people like Griswold and Buxton risk arrest to challenge the Connecticut law against contraception?

First, the Connecticut law affected its citizens unequally, and the split, simply put, was along class and racial lines. Well-informed women or women who could afford to go to private doctors willing to break the law had access to birth control. Because clinics could not operate openly in the state—they could be charged with aiding and abetting in the use of contraceptives—there were no low-cost family-planning facilities. As Harriet Pilpel, the general counsel for Planned Parenthood, put it: "The only way we could provide public access to contraception in those years was to have an underground railroad, transporting women in station wagons to Rhode Island or New York to get contraceptive materials."[6]

Second, the Connecticut law was the most stringent in the United States. In 1929, twenty-nine states had laws forbidding the dissemination of information about birth control. Because Connecticut outlawed the *use*, and not just the distribution, of contraceptives, the law turned many ordinary married couples into criminal offenders. Moreover, like the laws of just nine other states—Arizona, Idaho, Kansas, Mississippi, Missouri, Montana, Nebraska, Pennsylvania, Washington—and the District of Columbia, the Connecticut law did not even allow for physicians to prescribe contraceptives when medically necessary to protect the health or the very lives of their patients.

Finally, the law represented control by the state over one of the most personal decisions a couple can make: whether and when to have a child. However, because proving that someone had illegally used birth control was practically impossible, the courts were not overflowing with convictions. As one Connecticut doctor put it, the law was "unenforceable short of having a policeman under every bed in the state."[7]

Even if, in practice, the law did not prevent couples from using birth control, opponents of the law, such as Griswold and Buxton, resented the symbolism of the state's outlawing so private a choice. They believed strongly that the law violated basic principles of fairness, autonomy, and privacy and could not be overlooked.

### A POWERFUL SYMBOL

By 1961, birth control had a long history of creating controversy in the United States. The roots of the controversy were complex. Birth control was, for many, more than merely the prevention of conception.

For feminists and social reformers, birth control represented a way for women to achieve emancipation from the physical and economic burdens of having too many or unwanted children. "Voluntary motherhood" was a revolutionary concept from the late 1800s that was meant to allow women to experience sexual freedom, remain in the workforce (and be economically independent from men if they chose), and take control of their lives.

For many whites, the question of limiting the number of children that were born inevitably led to questions about the *kind* of families that would be smaller. In the early 1900s, no less a figure than U.S. president Theodore Roosevelt condemned the use of birth control as a selfish act by women who were unconcerned about the possibility of "race suicide." This term was used by those who feared that the decrease in the size of white families would eventually lead to a nation populated by more nonwhites than whites.

For nonwhites and poor women, there was

ample reason to be skeptical about the enthusiasm to provide them with birth control. Birth control agencies that linked poverty relief with family-planning services, particularly when the government was involved, raised suspicions that birth control supporters were more interested in controlling the size of nonwhite, working-class populations than in "emancipating" them.

For the politically powerful Roman Catholic Church, birth control was, of course, immoral. The Church objects on moral grounds to all kinds of birth control except the "rhythm method." The rhythm method limits a couple's intercourse to those times when the woman is not ovulating and is thus less likely to become pregnant. A statement released in 1958 by the Archdiocese of New York explains this view: "The natural law commands that the married state, as ordained by God, fulfill the function of the conservation of the human race. Artificial birth control frustrates that purpose. It is, therefore, unnatural, since it is contrary to the nature and dignity of man in the exercise of his faculties and subverts the sacredness of marriage."

By 1961, opposition to changing or repealing the Connecticut law came largely from legislators who either were Catholic themselves or did not want to offend their large Catholic constituencies. An article in *Time* magazine estimated that in the early 1960s about 46 percent of Connecticut's population was Roman Catholic. In states such as Connecticut where the Church retained a dominant political presence, the fight over birth control took on great significance. State laws that followed Church teachings, such as the one that made birth control illegal, were evidence that the Church was still a powerful force. Reluctant to cede such authority, the Church was one of the main opponents of legalized contraception. There were, as well, members of the Catholic Church who agreed with those worried about "race suicide" and used this concern to support their position.

With the potent symbolism so many people attached to birth control, it is no wonder that the Connecticut law remained in effect so long. The law was not a popular one—as early as the 1930s, most of Connecticut's citizens favored legal birth control—but it was supported by powerful political forces.

Some twenty-three attempts to reform or repeal the law were brought before the Connecticut legislature. Lawyers and birth control supporters also combined forces on several occasions to test the validity of the law in court. However, before *Griswold v. Connecticut* was decided by the U.S. Supreme Court, no one had been able to overturn the law. Indeed, just months before the arrest of Griswold and Buxton, the Supreme Court had dismissed a case challenging the constitutionality of the same Connecticut statute. In that case, Supreme Court justice Felix Frankfurter noted that although the law was still on the books, no one had been charged with violating it for years. Because there was no "fear of enforcement" of the law, there was also no reason to decide a case concerning its impact. The Supreme Court could not, he explained, "be umpire to debates concerning harmless, empty shadows."[8]

By opening the New Haven clinic in November 1961, Planned Parenthood set out to test whether the Connecticut law was merely an "empty shadow." If it was, the clinic would be able to serve its clients without interference from the authorities. If, on the other hand, the law was enforced and arrests made, birth control supporters would challenge the law before the Supreme Court of the United States. It was the best they could hope for.

*Anthony Comstock, the leader of a turn-of-the-century crusade against obscene materials in society*

# Chapter 2

# EARLY CRUSADERS
# AND REFORMERS

The Connecticut law that Estelle Griswold sought to overturn dates back to 1879. It began with a controversial man named Anthony Comstock.

Comstock was a colorful crusader, easily identified by his long, bushy sideburns, which stood in stark contrast to his round, bald head. He became a household name in the late 1800s and early 1900s by railing against the evils he saw in society. The "Comstock laws," named after him, were federal and state laws that prohibited the distribution of the broad sweep of items that Comstock considered obscene and immoral. These included contraceptive devices as well as pornography and "lewd" writings. *Comstockery* was a term that, as Comstock himself defined it, meant using "the noblest principles of law . . . in the interest of public morals."[1]

Born in 1844 to Puritan parents, Anthony Comstock was schooled in religion as a young boy. Later, when he was grown, he was both disgusted by and obsessed with the political corruption, gambling, prostitution, and poverty that he saw while working as a salesman in New York City. A diary entry illustrates his torment: "If I could but live without sin, I should be the happiest soul living: but Sin, that foe that is ever lurking, stealing happiness from me."[2] Comstock sought refuge from temptation in the Young Men's Christian Association (YMCA). In time, and with that organization's financial support, he was able to devote himself to his particular passion: stopping the trade of all sinful items, including contraceptives.

Birth control in Comstock's time was a poorly understood process. Little was known about the female reproductive cycle, and manipulating substances and timing to prevent pregnancy was often more of an art than a science. Advertisements for contraception were plentiful, but reliable sources of detailed information were few. The printed matter that existed explaining birth control methods, and doctors themselves, tended to be discreetly vague. The best hope for many was that friends and older relatives would give sound advice on how to prevent pregnancy.

Condoms made from animal membranes had been available for some time, but they were too expensive for most people to use. In 1837, Charles Goodyear, a Connecticut inventor, developed the rubber condom using a process known as vulcanization. Suddenly, it was possible to mass-produce a cheap, fairly reliable method of birth control.

With the advent of readily available contraception, two opposing movements emerged. Some considered birth control beneficial; by controlling family size, birth control fought against poverty among the urban poor. Others saw it as an accessory to immoral behavior and believed it should be eradicated from society. Anthony Comstock was decidedly in the latter camp.

In 1873, Comstock lobbied Congress for the passage of his "Comstock Act." He was fully supported by the YMCA, antivice societies, church groups, and temperance leagues, organizations that promoted abstinence from alcohol and other "sinful" activities and influences. At congressional hearings, Comstock showed legislators the sorts of items that contributed to social decay: pornographic literature and contraceptives. The evidence he presented was not scientific, but it proved persuasive. With virtually no opposition, the legislation, known officially as the Act for the Suppression of Trade in and Circulation of Obscene Literature and Articles of Immoral Use, became law one month later. The law banned sending certain materials through the U.S. mail, including every

> *obscene, lewd, or lascivious book, pamphlet, picture, paper, print, or other publication of an indecent character, or . . . article or thing designed or intended for the prevention of conception or procuring of abortion . . . [and] any article or thing intended or adapted for any indecent or immoral use or nature.*[3]

After Congress passed the federal Comstock Act, there were calls for the enactment of similar laws in every state legislature. Comstock and his antivice squads went to work. Their campaign ended with the passage of obscenity legislation that included restrictions on birth control in over half the states.

In 1879, the legislature of Connecticut, Comstock's home state, introduced a bill to outlaw trafficking in "obscene" materials concerning sex or

Anthony Comstock: "Arrest them all—The laws of decency must be respected!"

*This political cartoon of the time parodies Comstock and his mission.*

reproduction—the Act to Amend an Act Concerning Offenses against Decency, Morality, and Humanity. Interestingly, the legislature's Joint Committee on Temperance was headed by a representative from Bridgeport, Connecticut, Phineas T. Barnum, a man better known to most for his world-class circus than for his political service. Although Comstock took credit for the bill, Barnum was responsi-

*Circus owner and legislator, P. T. Barnum
towers over his celebrity midget, Tom Thumb,
in this famous photograph.*

ble for adding language to it that prohibited the *use* of "any drug, medicinal article or instrument whatsoever for the purpose of preventing conception."[4] When the legislature passed the act with little debate, Connecticut became the only state in the country that forbade the actual use and not just distribution of contraceptives. Needless to say, enforcement of such a law would prove difficult, if not impossible.

### MARGARET SANGER: CHAMPION OF WOMEN'S FREEDOM

If Anthony Comstock's mission had been to pass laws restricting behavior, then Margaret Sanger's was to undo that same work. Known today as an outspoken champion of a woman's right to control her own childbearing, Margaret Sanger fought for more than fifty years to end the injustice that, she believed, grew from the combination of poverty and the absence of reproductive choice. Sanger became an advocate for social change whose crusade was, as she put it, to "free women from incessant child bearing . . . [and] undesired pregnancy." If women had access to safe and reliable methods of preventing pregnancy, Sanger argued, the condition of their own lives as well as that of society would be advanced. At the time, her views were extremely controversial and provoked political groups from all sides. Some critics thought the behavior that Sanger advocated was intolerably liberal, while others viewed popular access to birth control as an attack on the growth of poor and nonwhite populations.

Margaret Sanger was born the sixth of eleven children in 1879. Her mother, a quiet woman who worked hard to meet the needs of her household, died of tuberculosis when Sanger was just fifteen. Sanger described her father, a stonemason who

*Margaret Sanger poses with her son Stuart in 1908.*

preferred talking and drinking to working, as a "tyrant," a "philosopher, a rebel, and an artist."[5] Although she resented her father's failings and the toll that she believed his behavior had taken on her mother, Sanger revered him for his compassion and enjoyment of life. She inherited his rebellious free spirit and his enthusiasm for radical causes. In her father, these characteristics made it difficult to keep a job; in Margaret Sanger, they were the traits that let her speak her mind and lent passion to her endeavors.

As a young woman, Sanger aspired to be a doctor. However, she was unable to afford the tuition, so at the age of fifteen she enrolled in nursing school at White Plains Hospital, outside of New York City. It was a disappointment for her. At that time nurses were not very well paid and performed many menial tasks, such as emptying bedpans, changing bed linens, cleaning, and cooking. In status, they were closer to domestic servants than medical professionals.

It was during those years as a nurse, however, that Sanger's inspiration to fight for women's reproductive freedom developed. She often recalled the tale of a young immigrant named Sadie Sachs who asked her doctor for contraception and was told to have her husband sleep on the roof. Three months later, Sanger left Sachs's side, unable to watch as her patient lay dying from a self-induced abortion. Margaret described what she called her "Great Awakening":

> *I looked out my window and down upon the dimly lighted city. Its pains and griefs crowded in upon me . . . women writhing in travail to bring forth little babies; the babies themselves naked and hungry, wrapped in newspapers to keep them from the cold; six-year-old children with pinched, pale wrinkled faces, old in concentrated wretchedness, pushed into gray and fetid cellars, crouching on stone floors, their small scrawny hands scuttling through rags. . . . I could bear it no longer. . . .*
>
> *As I stood there the darkness faded. The sun came up and threw its reflection over the house tops. It was the dawn of a new day in my life also. . . .*
>
> *I was resolved to seek out the root of the evil, to do something to change the destiny of mothers whose miseries were as vast as the sky.*[6]

And so Margaret Sanger's crusade was launched.

Sanger began her campaign in 1914 with a radical monthly paper called the *Woman Rebel*. "No Gods, No Masters" read the banner across the top of the first issue. In her paper, Sanger attacked the Comstock laws, motherhood, and marriage.

After the first issue, the U.S. Post Office warned her to stop publishing, but she defied it. She was charged with violating the Comstock laws by using the mail to "incite murder and assassination" and to circulate "obscene" literature, that is, information about birth control. She fled to Europe to avoid standing trial but, before she left, drafted *Family Limitation*, a sixteen-page procontraception pamphlet. The charges against Sanger were eventually dropped, but her husband spent thirty days in prison for distributing his wife's publication to a government agent.

Margaret Sanger's writings caused her to collide with Anthony Comstock at least once. It was over a column that Sanger wrote for the *Call*, a Socialist daily newspaper. Sanger's column, "What Every Girl Should Know," talked frankly about reproduction and sexuality. When the column took up the subject of syphilis, Comstock, as U.S. Post Office censor, stepped in and banned the column. In response, the paper saved the space and printed the headline: "What Every Girl Should Know— Nothing; by order of the U.S. Post Office." The column did appear some weeks later.

After a year abroad, Sanger returned to the United States in October 1915. During her time overseas, Anthony Comstock died, at age seventy-one, either of pneumonia or of "overdoing in a purity convention."[7]

## THE FIRST PUBLIC BIRTH CONTROL CLINICS

On October 16, 1916, Sanger and her sister Ethel Byrne, also a nurse, opened the first public birth control clinic in the United States. On its first day, forty-five women stood in line outside the Brooklyn storefront tenement house waiting for an appointment to receive information about birth control and sexuality for a ten-cent fee. The clinic had no doctor and did not even dispense contraceptive devices.

Nine days after the clinic's opening, police arrested Sanger, an assistant, and eventually her sister Ethel. They also impounded the clinic's supplies and patient records.

Sanger spent the night in jail. She opened the clinic again after a few weeks, but it was raided a second time and Sanger was charged with maintaining a public nuisance. Margaret Sanger and Ethel Byrne were convicted in a noisy courtroom filled with their supporters. Poor mothers whom Sanger had served at the clinic, many clutching infants and children, sat side by side with the fashionably attired, wealthy women of the National Birth Control League, America's first birth control advocacy group. "Shame!" was the response uttered by Sanger when her sentence, a $5,000 fine or thirty days in the workhouse, was finally announced.[8]

In 1921, Sanger again broke new ground when she convened the first American Birth Control Conference in New York City. One reason for organizing the conference was to attract publicity for the cause, which it certainly did. The New York City police, claiming that they were acting under orders from the Catholic archbishop of New York, raided the meeting, lending an air of excitement to an otherwise dull conference. Margaret Sanger was led away carrying long-stemmed red roses as the band played "My Country 'Tis of Thee." Press coverage, mostly critical of the raid, promoted the birth control movement. As a result of the melee, the *New Republic* reported, "the outlook for the birth

Above: *America's first public birth control clinic opened in this Brooklyn tenement in 1916* Inset: *Ethel Byrne (shown with a patient) and her sister Margaret Sanger met with clients here to discuss birth control methods.*

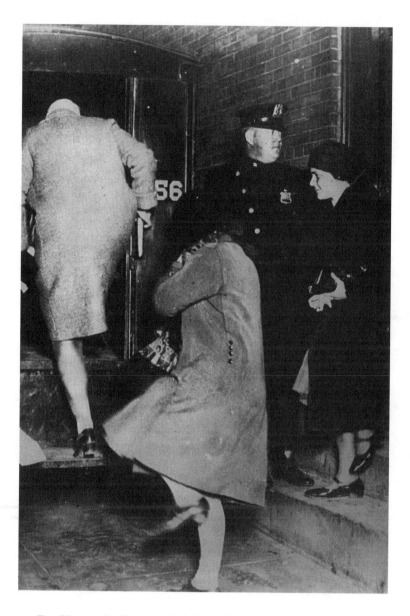

*Dr. Hannah Stone (right) and her staff at the Birth
Control Clinical Research Bureau were led into a
police paddy wagon after a raid in 1929.*

control movement is brighter than it ever was." An investigation into the affair never produced an admission by the Catholic Church that it was behind the disruption. One thing was certain: it would not be the last time birth control advocates and the leadership of the Catholic Church would clash.

The conference also served as the kickoff for the American Birth Control League (ABCL), a national organization that would soon have state and local offices. Its goals reflected Margaret Sanger's agenda: to educate the public about women's health, advocate repeal of the Comstock laws, sponsor medical research, and provide advice about birth control. The organization reached hundreds of thousands of women through the pamphlets, letters, books, and copies of the *Birth Control Review*, distributed by mostly white, well-educated, middle-class or wealthy volunteers.

Although the ABCL had affiliates across the country, Sanger concentrated her own efforts largely in New York City, particularly around the Birth Control Clinical Research Bureau, which she founded in 1923. From modest beginnings and under the careful leadership of Dr. Hannah Stone, the clinic grew and thrived despite the constraints of the law. Stone and her team of doctors prescribed birth control to married women with a medical need for it. Women engaged to be married and other patients who did not satisfy the legal criteria were quietly given referrals to private physicians. By the end of the 1920s, the clinic was seeing some 5,000 new patients per year and had seen nearly 20,000 in all, more than all the other birth control centers in the rest of the United States.[9]

Other birth control facilities existed in a few cities scattered across the country. During the 1920s, clinics opened in New York, Cleveland,

*Just days after the 1929 raid, Margaret Sanger was officially censored with adhesive tape to keep her from preaching birth control at a meeting in Boston.*

Chicago, Detroit, and Los Angeles. For the most part, they were poorly funded, faced powerful opposition, and encountered difficulty in getting supplies. As a result, they served only a small percentage of women who wanted their services.

## CAMPAIGNS TO REFORM CONNECTICUT'S COMSTOCK LAW

At the same time, in Connecticut, the state that would be the site of Estelle Griswold's battle, birth control activists were on the threshold of a long fight to pass a bill reforming the restrictive Comstock law in the legislature. Each of their attempts, which spanned decades of legislative sessions, ultimately failed. Their biennial campaigns to change the law were, however, the centerpiece of the birth control movement in Connecticut during the years before *Griswold* was decided.

Margaret Sanger was very much at the center of the first campaign to reform Connecticut's "little Comstock law," in 1923. Most of the groundwork for the campaign was done by local supporters of her American Birth Control League. But it was Margaret Sanger who rallied the crowd at Parson's Theater in Hartford on the Sunday before the legislative hearing. Over 800 supporters, mostly women, listened to Sanger's call to free women from the burdens of childbearing and for legal birth control under medical supervision.

Representatives of the Roman Catholic Church made up the strongest opposition to the bill. They spoke after Sanger, presenting a host of arguments rooted in the doctrine of the Church: birth control was a violation of "natural law," and sex for a purpose other than procreation was a "perversion of that function." The auxiliary bishop, John G. Murray, also called for the preservation of the race, arguing that unless they had four children per family, "the races from northern Europe . . . the finest type of people, are doomed to extinction." Sanger rebutted with sarcasm: "The gentlemen say that it is against the laws of nature to prevent conception, yet they themselves are celibates."[10] Despite the apparent popular support for Sanger's position, the bill was rejected by both houses in the state legislature some weeks later.

In 1925, Sanger's reformers brought their second bill before the Connecticut legislature. In addition to a medical doctor and Sanger, Katharine Houghton Hepburn, a well-known activist in birth control and women's suffrage movements and mother of the movie star, spoke before the crowd of 100. The sole speaker from the opposition represented the Connecticut Council of Catholic Women. She warned her listeners sternly: "Persons shouldn't enter into the married life unless they are willing to accept the obligation of children." She argued, "There is already too much love of luxury and ease and this bill would encourage that very thing." Although the hearings went well for birth control advocates, the bill was swiftly defeated.[11]

By 1927, enthusiasm for birth control activism was on the wane. ABCL membership fell from 13,000 members in 1923 to 2,800 in 1926. The *Birth Control Review* had only forty-seven subscribers in all of Connecticut.

After another defeat in the legislature that year, ABCL organizers set up local birth control committees in small towns to muster support for reform. The method was so effective that they garnered the endorsement of the conference of Congregational churches in Connecticut for the 1929 hearing. That year, the hearing was raucous, with nearly 1,000 people in attendance.

*John G. Murray, the auxiliary bishop of the Catholic Church who opposed the 1923 bill to reform Connecticut's "little Comstock law"*

*Katharine H. Hepburn, a birth control activist who supported the bill to reform Connecticut's "little Comstock law"*

Katharine H. Hepburn stirred the crowd. She began by claiming, "Three quarters of the men and women in this room are common criminals and ought to be in jail. . . . The crime is in having too many children where parents are too poor, too unintelligent to raise many children, in raising children that can never be adjusted to society." She ended with a sharp attack on the Catholic Church, the main source of opposition to the bill: "Roman Catholic women are coming to realize that this is their concern and not that of their priests; that they, and not the priests, have to bear the children."[12]

Opponents of the bill chastised the birth control supporters, implying that their position was irresponsible. "Let them practice self-control, not birth control!" thundered one legislator. "If they want the sex relationship, let them take what goes with it," was the message of the opposition's leader, the father of nine children.[13]

The bill was eventually defeated without debate in the state senate. It was, however, debated on the floor of the house of representatives, which was a first for the cause. Representative Epaphroditus Peck, a lawyer, forced the floor debate and was the main supporter of the bill. He decried the statute as religious legislation supported by a Roman Catholic bloc and pointed out that no prosecutions had ever been made under the law. One female state representative spoke against the bill, arguing that if it passed, only immigrants would contribute to population growth and girls could become prostitutes and "seventy-five per cent of them will."[14] Her statements were met with such a swell of hissing, she was silenced as she stood. Nevertheless, the bill was defeated by a landslide of 226 to 18.

In 1930, encouraging news for birth control
supporters came from the federal judiciary. The
U.S. Court of Appeals for the Second Circuit decided *Young's Rubber Co. v. C. I. Lee and Co.*, holding
that it was not illegal to transport condoms if they
were to be used after being prescribed by a physician where local laws permitted. With this powerful statement in favor of a "doctor's exception" to
restrictions on birth control, Connecticut reformers
planned to introduce a "doctors' bill" in the 1931
legislative session. The group, working under the
name of the Connecticut Birth Control League
(CBCL), enlisted the support of more than 400
Connecticut physicians.

In a surprising break from the nearly routine
rejection of any birth control law reform bill, the judiciary committee endorsed an amended bill that
would allow doctors to prescribe birth control but
only for specific health needs. Even in amended
form, the bill was defeated by a hefty margin in
both houses.

The fact that the Connecticut judiciary committee had even considered the 1931 doctors' bill
raised birth control supporters' hopes of an eventual victory. After the hearing, there was renewed enthusiasm and an increase in CBCL membership.
Several male doctors, determined to lay a foundation for the next legislative push, suggested a reor-
ganization of the CBCL and an outreach into
Connecticut's cities and towns to drum up popular
support for passing a reform bill. Toward this end,
one gynecologist, A. Nowell Creadick, successfully
petitioned the Connecticut State Medical Society to
issue a statement of unanimous support. A few
days later, he was elected president of the CBCL.

In light of the regular setbacks in the legislature, it is puzzling that the birth control advocates

did not turn to other methods to advance their cause. In the debate over strategy, organizers did discuss nullification—a strategy that involved ignoring the law, opening clinics, distributing information and devices for contraception, and working to change public opinion. If the community solidly endorsed the availability of birth control, the reasoning went, then perhaps the law would go unenforced. League organizers in Providence, Rhode Island, opened New England's first public birth control clinic without incident in July 1931. The Connecticut organization under Creadick's leadership weighed the possibility of following suit but rejected the "flagrant violation" method. The unique feature of the Connecticut law that penalized the *use* of contraception was the deciding factor against the nullification approach.

In 1933, the reform bill advanced by the CBCL carved out an exception to the 1879 law to permit physicians to prescribe contraception when "in [their] opinion pregnancy would be detrimental to the health of the patient." Both the roster of speakers and the evidence were impressive and persuasive. Prominent physicians testified to the numbers of women who had died from pregnancy-related causes. Signatures of the thousands of supporters, including more than half the doctors in Connecticut, were submitted. The primary speaker for the bill, an officer of the Connecticut State Medical Society, attempted to remove the bill from the emotional fray, stating it was "purely [a] medical measure for the purpose of preserving the health of our women."[15]

The Connecticut house of representatives passed the bill with one slight amendment: it would apply only to married women. The margin of victory—169 to 80—was solid. Ratification, however, requires that both houses in the state legislature approve a bill, and the senate rejected it soundly.

The next legislative campaign, in 1935, was led by Sallie Pease, who replaced A. Nowell Creadick as president of the CBCL. The overwhelming public sentiment that reached legislators, mostly from Catholic districts, opposed reform. The judiciary committee reached a tie vote, and the bill sputtered out.

If it had not been clear earlier, the 1935 effort brought home the failure of the CBCL's attempts at legislative reform. Although each effort built on the lessons learned from the previous one, victory remained elusive.

## A CLINIC IN CONNECTICUT

After the legislative failure in 1935, an offer from a wealthy supporter to finance a clinic in Hartford lifted the spirits of CBCL members. The Hartford Maternal Health Center opened within a month. The clientele was narrowly defined: a patient had to be married, be living with her husband, have at least one child or be physically or economically unfit for pregnancy, and be unable to pay for private care. The restrictions tested the limits of the statute without outwardly aggravating the authorities.

Despite efforts to shield the clinic from watchful authorities, word of its opening eventually spread. After a report in the press, it became apparent that the clinic would not be shut down or its organizers arrested. A small number of clinics began to sprout in Connecticut.

Apparently content with their success in the field, if not on the statute books, the CBCL decided to sit out the 1937 legislative session in Connecticut. The doctors at the clinics were at least moving in the direction of fulfilling one aim of the League—making birth control and family-planning advice available to all women, and in this their efforts were obviously more successful than the League's attempts at legislative reform.

The shifting tactics of the CBCL were a response to the relaxed vigilance of the state and local authorities and the mood of the country in the mid-1930s. Although the Comstock laws remained valid, the distribution of birth control information and devices was common in publicly funded programs and businesses. Workers in relief agencies, particularly in areas of the country without a strong Catholic presence, were known to have referred clients in need of birth control to publicly funded clinics or physicians. Public funds directly supported clinics in Los Angeles, Virginia, and Missouri. In Miami, federal employees of the Works Progress Administration were even employed in maternal health clinics.

In the private sector, scrutiny of the distribution of contraceptives seemed negligible. One journal reported that the mailing of contraceptives was as common as "the use of a gummed postage stamp." "Preventives" were even available in the Sears, Roebuck catalog. None of these developments were apt to upset most Americans; polls in 1936 showed that 70 percent of Americans favored legalizing birth control.[16]

### *UNITED STATES v. ONE PACKAGE*

Formal change took place in 1936 when Anthony Comstock's federal legacy, the Act of 1873, was severely limited in *United States v. One Package*, a case that came before the U.S. Court of Appeals for the Second Circuit. *One Package* involved a package of contraceptives sent by a Japanese doctor to Margaret Sanger. When the package was confiscated by U.S. customs, Sanger asked the doctor to send it again, this time addressed to Dr. Hannah Stone, so that Sanger could set up a case to press for a medical exemption of the Comstock laws.

With one sweep of the judicial pen, the court handed down a medical exception in the federal law, very similar to the reform the Connecticut group had been fighting for in the state legislature for years. Judge Augustus Hand wrote that the Comstock Act encompassed

> *only such articles as Congress would have denounced as immoral if it had understood all the conditions under which they were to be used. Its design, in our opinion, was not to prevent the importation, sale, or carriage by mail of things which might intelligently be employed by conscientious and competent physicians for the purpose of saving life or promoting the well-being of their patients.*[17]

The national press heralded the decision and Margaret Sanger's efforts. Sanger's lawyer, Morris Ernst, hailed the decision as "the end of birth control laws." He expected that the eight states that had birth control laws without the so-called doctor's exception would follow *One Package*'s lead. Katharine Hepburn agreed: "I think we should say we have won."[18]

And so the League did not challenge Anthony Comstock's laws in the Connecticut legislature in 1937. After *One Package*, there seemed no need. Clinic organizers throughout the state simply bypassed, or flat out ignored the laws.

Was the battle over? Did *One Package* mean that the Connecticut Birth Control League could, at last, declare victory and end its biennial struggle against the state legislature? The decision in *One Package* was encouraging, and birth control clinics were open and busy—the Hartford clinic alone had seen nearly 700 new patients in one year—and expanding. Anthony Comstock's law, however, was still on the books in Connecticut, and a long, long road lay ahead.

*In 1938, the Connecticut Birth Control League set up a birth control clinic in the Chase Dispensary at Waterbury Hospital.*

# Chapter 3

# TESTING CONNECTICUT LAW

**W**ith the legislative battle in Connecticut placed aside, reformers turned to expanding the League's small network of clinics. Under the direction of CBCL president Sallie Pease, two supporters of the cause—a nurse, Clara McTernan, and a field worker, Leah Cadbury—set to work opening a birth control clinic in Waterbury.

They selected the Chase Dispensary building at Waterbury Hospital as the clinic site. Then they signed on two doctors. William Goodrich, a Columbia Medical School graduate and a friend of McTernan's family, would be the lead doctor of the Waterbury team. Having worked as an intern in the Hartford Maternal Health Center after medical school, he was familiar with the politics of birth control. Goodrich brought in the second doctor, a Cornell Medical School graduate named Roger Nelson. McTernan also arranged for three women to assist in running the clinic.

Then McTernan took the fateful step of formally requesting the use of two rooms one day a week at the hospital. The request included the usual restrictions on birth control clinics at the time: birth control services would be given only to married women who were living with their husbands and could not afford private medical care. Most important, the hospital and the center would be distinct entities with no connection, especially of a financial nature, between the two. All funds for supplies and maintenance would come from volunteers, not hospital coffers.

Clinic service in the Waterbury Maternal Health Center began on October 11, 1938, about eight months after Clara McTernan had first volunteered for the cause. Business was moderate; during one week, the clinic might serve only ten to twelve patients, some of whom had given birth to four or five children in as many years.

## REACTION TO THE WATERBURY CLINIC

Six months later, when Sallie Pease gave her president's report at the annual CBCL meeting, she highlighted the success of the Waterbury clinic, the first Connecticut clinic to operate in a public institution. After twelve years of campaigning in the legislature, she noted, the CBCL had found relatively quick success by simply opening clinics. Pease made these seemingly harmless remarks at a luncheon on Thursday, June 8, 1939.

The next day's headline of the *Waterbury Democrat* marked the beginning of a chain of events that would be a setback for the birth control movement. "Birth Control Clinic Is Operating In City," the *Democrat* reported. The newspaper of choice for much of Waterbury's substantial Roman Catholic population, the *Democrat* shared the Catholic Church's firm opposition to birth control.

The Church reacted quickly. By Saturday morning, Catholic clergy had drafted a strongly worded resolution opposing the clinic and warning Catholics to stay away from it. The resolution also called for an investigation and, if appropriate, prosecution by the authorities "to the full extent of the law."[1] The resolution was not published until Monday morning, but Catholics throughout Waterbury had a preview of the Church's stance. On Sunday morning, it was read from the pulpit of every Roman Catholic church in Waterbury.

One churchgoer who heard the resolution was the recently appointed state's attorney for Waterbury, Bill Fitzgerald. A thirty-seven-year-old Harvard Law School graduate, Fitzgerald was known equally for his intelligence and his devotion to the Church. It was his job to enforce the laws of Connecticut, whether they were old-fashioned and unpopular or not. Furthermore, he had recently witnessed a vivid example of the consequences of failing to carry out the responsibilities of that position. His predecessor, Larry Lewis, had been forced to resign for failing to enforce the state's gambling laws. With Lewis's fate in mind, Fitzgerald decided to investigate the Waterbury clinic.

On the Monday morning that the Church's resolution was published, Fitzgerald applied to Judge Frank McEvoy for a warrant to search the Chase Dispensary. The judge was well acquainted with the politics of birth control. Described by one colleague as "wildly Irish Catholic," he had grown up with the teachings of the Church and was married to an outspoken opponent of birth control. Seven years earlier, his wife had fought to stop the League of Women Voters from endorsing birth control at its state convention and threatened that "she and all Catholic women would resign" if the group voted to support legalizing birth control. Thus, fully aware of the social and the legal concerns surrounding the issue, McEvoy approved without hesitation Bill Fitzgerald's request for a warrant to search the Chase Dispensary for "books, records, registers, instruments, apparatus and appliances" that were being used to violate Connecticut's birth control laws.[2]

### AN INVESTIGATION

It was still early, just before 10:00 A.M., when an assistant at the clinic showed the deputy sheriff and a county detective the two rooms in the dispensary where the clinic operated. After they searched the rooms, the law officers left carrying part of what they had come for. Although they had several bags filled with contraceptive devices, they were missing an important piece of the investigation: the patient records. Those documents were in the hands of Virginia Goss, a clinic worker, and she would not give them up without a bit of a chase.

Goss had been tipped off by a friend who knew the state's attorney was looking for the clinic's patient records. In an attempt to protect the clinic and its patients, Goss took the patient cards and fled to her summer home, off the coast of Connecticut. After a call from an attorney, the drama ended quickly, and Goss returned to Waterbury with the records and handed them over to Fitzgerald.

A hearing was held before Judge McEvoy. Coincidentally, Fitzgerald stood opposite Larry Lewis, his former boss, in the courtroom that day. Lewis, the state's attorney who had resigned amidst scandal, was now working with attorney Warren Upson to defend the clinic and the CBCL. The coincidences of the case did not end there. After Judge McEvoy had examined the evidence taken from the clinic and pressed the clinic's attorneys to reveal the names of the clinic's officers, three women were named, including Virginia Goss and Clara McTernan, a friend and next-door neighbor for many years of Bill Fitzgerald.

That afternoon, Fitzgerald undertook the awkward job of interrogating his friend about her involvement with the clinic she had founded. What did Waterbury Hospital's board of directors know about the clinic? Had McTernan ever spoken to them? Who was on the Waterbury Committee? Who had donated money? Who attended meetings about the clinic? By the time Fitzgerald had finished questioning McTernan and Goss, he had a clear picture of who was involved with the clinic and the roles they played.

While other women's health clinics across Connecticut were open for business as usual, Clara McTernan and doctors William Goodrich and Roger Nelson appeared before Judge Kenneth Wynne of the Connecticut Superior Court—the state's trial court—and were charged with violating Connecticut's birth control law. Specifically, McTernan and Goodrich were charged with providing birth control to three women: "a twenty-two-year-old mother of two who had visited the dispensary no fewer than forty-four times for a variety of illnesses in less than four years, a twenty-two-year-old mother who had borne three children within three years, and a twenty-three-year-old mother who had borne four children within four years." Nelson faced similar charges involving three different women. All three defendants pleaded not guilty. Acknowledging that they were "acting in accordance with what they think they have a right to do," Wynne released the three defendants into the custody of their lawyer Larry Lewis.[3]

According to one report, the arrests left Goodrich and Nelson "panic-stricken." Newly in practice with families to support, the two young doctors were understandably anxious about the arrests. If convicted, they could lose their medical licenses.

## IN THE TRIAL COURT

In the case involving the charges against McTernan, Goodrich, and Nelson—known as *State v. Nelson*—Warren Upson filed a demurrer. This legal device is used when the defendants do not deny the charges against them. "Yes, we did it," they argue, "but we are not guilty because the law is unconstitutional. We can not be punished for breaking a law that itself violates the Constitution."

Upson's briefs—the legal documents that contained his arguments—were forcefully written. He began by describing the original purpose of the 1879 statute and explaining to the court why it did not apply to the activities of the clinic. The law had been written "to prohibit the production and dissemination of obscene information and literature." While distribution of contraceptives to some groups, high school girls, for instance, may be considered immoral, he argued, "any use of a contraceptive device upon the advice of a physician is not an offense against morality."[4]

Upson then put forth his primary argument: that married people had a "natural right," one that is not granted by the government, the Constitution, or the Bill of Rights, to decide if and when they would have children. Because it stood in the way of that right, the 1879 law was an "unconstitutional interference with the individual liberty of the citizens of Connecticut." The law was especially egregious because there was no exception in the law to protect even those patients whose life or health was at risk. "If the people of Connecticut have any natural rights whatsoever," he wrote, "one of them certainly is the right to decide whether or not they shall have children, and to this natural right, the right to use contraceptive devices is a natural concomitant. With the powers of the State ever encroaching upon the rights of its citizens, it is surely time for the courts to fix a point beyond which the State cannot go."[5]

Surprisingly, the judge agreed with Upson's conclusions and upheld the demurrer. Judge Wynne weighed the obligation of Connecticut's doctors to protect the health of their patients against the need of the state to protect its citizens from obscenity and immorality in the form of birth control devices and information. He reasoned that a doctor's mission was the more important of the two.

The decision was an unexpected victory for a movement that had grown accustomed to defeat, and birth control supporters were jubilant. Sallie Pease called it "a great triumph of common sense over a ridiculous" law. Clara McTernan was optimistic and full of praise for "the world's best lawyer." Looking ahead, she wrote to ask Upson when she should plan on reopening the clinic.

### THE APPEAL

Despite the early victory, celebration was premature. Not unexpectedly, Bill Fitzgerald appealed Judge Wynne's ruling. Oral arguments on the appeal were held before the five-member appeals court, the Connecticut Supreme Court of Errors.

Upson commented after the argument, "I am rather pessimistic about the outcome." Sallie Pease, who observed the hearing, was also aware that the justices did not accept Upson's arguments favorably. "We left with a sinking feeling in our hearts," she recalled later; the justices "seemed so old, so remote from the urgencies of life, so entangled in the musty depths of the law."[6]

There is a long-standing debate among legal scholars about how much authority courts should have to change how laws are interpreted and applied. One argument is that judges should be activists. That is, courts should use their authority to create social change even when legal precedent does not support them. The other argument is that judges should defer to the legislature. If a law is to be significantly changed or repealed, the argument goes, it is up to the legislature, not the judiciary, to do it. In the legislature, representatives who are elected by the people vote on a bill. If voters are dissatisfied with the decisions their legislators make, they can elect different representatives. In contrast, while some judges are elected, many are appointed and cannot be removed from their posts for writing unpopular opinions.

Three of the five judges of the court of appeals deferred to the legislature and rejected Judge Wynne's ruling. The opinion stated explicitly that the statute as it was written did not carve out an exception that allowed doctors to prescribe birth control. It was up to the legislature, not the court, to create one. In its ruling, the court emphasized that the failed attempts at legislative reform or repeal from 1923 to 1935 indicated that the voters did not want the bill repealed. They wrote, "rejection by the Legislature of a specific provision is most persuasive, that the act should not be construed to include it."

Sallie Pease and other CBCL members had been prepared for the unfavorable decision, which one member called "a disgrace to our state." Only hours after the decision was announced, Pease sent telegrams to each of the still-functioning clinics with the message, "I suggest it is advisable to close." None of the local groups disagreed. So after a brief respite from the law, on March 20, 1940, the poorer women and families of Connecticut were once again left without easy access to birth control or family-planning guidance.

With the clinics closed, Bill Fitzgerald chose not to prosecute McTernan, Goodrich, and Nelson. Generously citing their cooperation and their lack of criminal intent, Fitzgerald argued in favor of withdrawing the charges against them. "I am satisfied that these defendants believed that they had a right to do the acts referred to in the informations in these cases. They donated their time and services to what they regarded as a charitable work." He continued, "It seems to me unjust to destroy the professional careers of these physicians by a conviction."[7]

After the Waterbury clinic closed, Bill Goodrich went off to the military. He eventually left gynecology for radiology and practiced in Hartford, where he raised two children. Roger Nelson also left obstetrics, but for hospital administration. Clara McTernan continued to live amicably next to Bill Fitzgerald, the man who had prosecuted the case against her, for some years. Apparently, neither family bore any ill will. Fitzgerald once even apologized for what he had done. Later his son remembered his father taking no pleasure in what happened. "It was as if he had been 'kind of holding his nose' during the events of 1939 and 1940."[8]

## FOLLOWING DEFEAT: A NEW STRATEGY

While the defendants settled back into their lives, the decision—with its taste of victory followed by ultimate, undiluted defeat—seemed to leave the CBCL in a state of turmoil. Margaret Sanger responded by lashing out at the CBCL leadership and, in particular, Sallie Pease, with charges of incompetence and weakness. Others associated with the CBCL cast about for a new strategy. Should they open the clinics again, as the League's attorney, Morris Ernst, suggested? Or should they mount yet another aggressive legislative campaign, as others urged?

In the end, the CBCL leadership agreed to a two-pronged strategy. They would introduce a bill during the 1941 legislative session that would allow hospitals, not private doctors, to "prescribe contraceptive devices to meet health problems of married women." They would also try to find a case that would test the limits of the law. The lawsuit, legal advisers concluded, would have to involve a "married woman [who] would be very likely to lose her life" in pregnancy if she were denied access to birth control.[9]

Meanwhile, clinics were operating in most other states. In March 1940, only seven states in the country had no centers. Pushing for increased public involvement, the two premier birth control organizations, the American Birth Control League and the Birth Control Clinical Research Bureau, joined to create the Birth Control Federation of America. The goal of the new organization was to integrate birth control into the public health program of

*In 1941, the Connecticut legislature met to debate the repeal of its birth control law.*

every state. One year after the consolidation, 553 birth control centers, 40 percent of which received financial support from tax funding, were operating in forty-two states and Puerto Rico.

In Connecticut, attorney Fritz Wiggin was given the job of searching for a doctor who was willing to prescribe birth control illegally and risk his or her medical license and reputation to take part in a test case. The case was sure to generate publicity when it was filed. Tensions between birth control activists and leaders of the Catholic Church were at a feverish pitch. The executive director of the CBCL captured the mood in a report to birth control supporters in New York. "Catholic opposition," he told them, "is rising in the state like a tidal wave."[10]

### A TEST CASE

The doctor who filed the test case was Wilder Tileston. Dr. Tileston had three patients for whom pregnancy might prove life-threatening, and on March 20, 1941, exactly one year after Sallie Pease advised Connecticut clinics to close their doors, Tileston filed a complaint in Connecticut's trial court.

The three women, known in the legal proceeding by the fictitious names of Jane Doe, Mary Roe, and Sarah Hoe, represented a variety of difficulties associated with pregnancy. Jane Doe, a forty-one-year-old mother of five children, the youngest just two months old, had very high blood pressure and had been told by her doctor that she should not become pregnant again. Mary Roe was considerably younger but suffered from tuberculosis she had contracted five years previously. Were she to become pregnant, the effects of the disease would be serious and possibly fatal. The third woman, Sarah Hoe, had been weakened by three pregnancies in a short time. She was also in a dire financial situation, and another child would jeopardize the well-being of her family.

The initiation of the lawsuit was barely noticed by the press. It was soon eclipsed completely by heated hearings in the state legislature on the reform bill. The bill passed soundly in the Connecticut house of representatives, but was equally soundly defeated in the senate. Tempers were still hot when the battle was over. Looking ahead to the next legislative session, the League announced its plans for the "battle of 1943."

Meanwhile, Fritz Wiggin and the defendant, the New Haven County state's attorney, Abraham S. Ullman, had agreed not to have a trial. Instead, they went directly to the appeals court. Together they drafted a stipulation (a compilation of the facts agreed to by both sides) and argued only about the application of the law. The legal arguments took place in February 1942 before a small group of interested observers and a five-judge panel of the Connecticut appeals court.

Four months later, a 3-to-2 decision was rendered that firmly upheld the 1879 law. The court's rationale was straightforward: the legislature had solidly supported the law since its inception and had never carved out an exception regarding the mother's health, and overturning the law was not up to the courts. The court wrote that the issue in the case was

> *whether abstinence from intercourse is a reasonable and practicable method of preventing the unfortunate consequences. . . . Do the frailties of human nature and the uncertainties of human passions render it impracticable?*

Its response:

*That is a question for the legislature, and we cannot say it could not believe that the husband and wife would and should refrain when they both knew that intercourse would very likely result in a pregnancy which might bring about the death of the wife.*[11]

At this stage of the proceedings, the only court that could hear an appeal of the decision was the U.S. Supreme Court. The appeal and its opposition were filed in August 1942, and the Supreme Court voted to hear the appeal in November. The Court's acceptance of the case boosted the spirits of Connecticut activists.

Any hopes that had been pinned on *Tileston v. Ullman* were soon dashed, however, by a fatal flaw in the way the case was filed. On appeal, it was the Supreme Court's role to determine whether the plaintiff's constitutional rights were violated by the 1879 law. The complaint filed in the Connecticut court asserted that the lives of the three women who were being denied birth control by the law were in jeopardy. The plaintiff—the person who filed the lawsuit asking for relief—named in the case, however, was Dr. Tileston, not Jane Doe, Mary Roe, and Sarah Hoe. Although the lives of the patients were quite possibly at risk, Dr. Tileston's was not. In short, Dr. Tileston did not have "standing" to bring the suit and challenge a law that did not affect him. The Supreme Court had no choice but to dismiss the appeal.

After the Supreme Court defeat, the CBCL's focus shifted back to the legislature. Ever persistent, the Connecticut League mounted a campaign for the 1943 session. But the next ten-year period, from 1943 to 1953, saw a dispiriting lag in the Connecticut birth control movement. After *Tileston*, a bill to change the Connecticut law was introduced and defeated at every state legislative session.

A new strategy was needed. There would be one, and Estelle Griswold would be the driving force behind it.

# Chapter 4

# CASE DISMISSED: A "HARMLESS, EMPTY SHADOW"

**P**hooey" was Estelle Griswold's first response. It was the fall of 1953 and Jennie Heiser, a fundraiser for the Planned Parenthood League of Connecticut (PPLC), had just asked Griswold to take over as executive director of the organization. (In 1942, the name of the national group was changed from the Birth Control Federation of America to the Planned Parenthood Federation of America, and the Connecticut organization followed suit, becoming the Planned Parenthood League of Connecticut.) A chance encounter led to the offer. Griswold lived next door to Planned Parenthood's offices on Trumbull Street in New Haven and had fallen into a conversation with Heiser. Griswold's answer would change, not because of a passion for the cause, but because, in her own words, she needed a paying job "very desperately."

Born Estelle Trebert in 1900, Griswold has been described by Catherine Roraback, the lawyer who represented her in the Supreme Court case that bore her name, as a "very dynamic woman, and I mean woman, with a capital W."[1] Raised in a Catholic family of modest means, Estelle Griswold was, by all accounts, determined, spirited, and talented. Although she did well enough in her Hartford public school classes to skip two grades, "Stelle" was not a model student. In high school, she was suspended for playing hookey and recruiting others to join her. After high school, Stelle watched her wealthier friends go off to college. She lacked the money to do the same. Instead, at twenty-two, she moved to Paris, hoping to become a singer. It was the first time she had ever left Hartford.

Estelle had an adventure-filled stay in France, where she did office work to support herself, learned to swear in French, was engaged to a playwright, and sang in the American Cathedral. When she learned that her mother was ill, Estelle returned home. Both of her parents died while Estelle was living in Hartford, doing office work to pay her bills and auditioning for singing jobs. After their deaths, she traveled for six months with a show group and returned to Hartford.

In 1927, her life changed again when she decided to marry Richard Griswold, a fellow graduate of Hartford High School who had gone to Yale University. As newlyweds, Dick and Estelle lived in the suburbs of New York City. Dick worked for a life insurance company in Manhattan, and Estelle sang for radio. When Estelle's singing tutor died in 1935, so did her dreams of having a singing career.

In 1945, World War II ended and the Griswolds found themselves caught in the swirl of global change. Estelle and Dick left to work in Europe for the next five years. Often they did not live in the same city. She worked for the United Nations and

**61**

Christian relief agencies in London, Holland, and Germany, helping refugees from the war relocate and resettle. This experience and her visits to the countries where she placed people gave Estelle an understanding of the problems of overpopulation. As she put it:

> *I saw poor, hungry people in the slums of Favola in Rio de Janeiro, in the La Perla area of Puerto Rico and Algiers.*
>
> *You think of people as civilized. . . . [E]ach human being living in comfort and wealth feels he is a dignified individual. A look at the slums of the world, at the chaos of a war-scorched earth, and you realize that life at the point of survival, where food, water and shelter are unobtainable, is close to reversion to an animal order. Survival is first; civilization is second.[2]*

After returning from overseas, the Griswolds settled into a handsome townhouse at 40 Trumbull Street in New Haven, Connecticut, next to the Planned Parenthood headquarters. At the time Jennie Heiser approached her, Griswold was executive secretary for an organization called the New Haven Human Relations Council. It was a good position but had ceased to be a paying one.

Griswold had never been particularly interested in the birth control movement. In fact, when she heard from her friend, Hilda Standish, about her position as executive director of the Hartford maternal health clinic, Griswold was ambivalent about the cause. "It just left me cold," she remembered. "I wanted children and hadn't been able to have them."[3] In fact, she admitted later that when she had her first serious conversations with a PPLC official about being executive director of the prominent birth control advocacy group, she had never seen a diaphragm and was not sure what it was.

Despite her ignorance about the details, Griswold's qualifications and prior experiences impressed the PPLC officers she spoke with, and the board quickly voted to offer her the job of executive director.

Meanwhile, Griswold was researching PPLC. Hilda Standish, who remembered well the era of Katharine Hepburn and Sallie Pease, told her bluntly, "[The PPLC is] practically dead. . . . If you really want to work your head off and get it above ground and going again, there's no better place to work." Those words may have discouraged some, but not Estelle Griswold. Standish recalled that, "she was that type of person; that was just the thing that set her off."[4] Griswold accepted the job in December 1953.

### ESTELLE GRISWOLD: WORKING TOWARD "SUCCESS IN OUR TIME"

Directing the Planned Parenthood that Estelle Griswold inherited was, indeed, challenging. There were financial worries, a history of failed attempts to change the law, and a grim outlook for legal birth control in Connecticut anytime soon. Griswold acknowledged this predicament, but she also saw the contribution she could make. "We have a long way to go," she said, "before we make a real impact on the public. It is somewhat discouraging at times, but . . . if we keep in mind the work that gave us our Constitution, the Emancipation Proclamation, the UN, votes for women and many other privileges that we accept for granted today, we should continue to work for our cause. We may not have 'success in our time,' but we may help to achieve it for future generations."[5]

In 1955, PPLC backed another failed attempt to pass a birth control bill in the Connecticut senate. Griswold, in response, began to turn her efforts toward other programs. Her immediate goal was to make sure that Planned Parenthood was serving the community by helping "women, for health or economic reasons, to regulate the size of their families."[6]

In Port Chester, New York, just across the border from Greenwich, Connecticut, Planned Parenthood of Eastern Westchester operated a birth control clinic. Griswold, along with Claudia McGinley, the new PPLC president, came up with the idea of widely advertising a program that would serve Connecticut women by referring them to the New York clinic. Volunteers would staff an office in Norwalk, Connecticut, and make appointments for Connecticut women at the New York clinic. They would also make "border runs," transporting women across the Connecticut–New York state line. The program, which received some funding from a spermicide manufacturer, began officially on April 10, 1956. Finally, members of the Planned Parenthood League of Connecticut could see the tangible results of their efforts.

The program did have drawbacks. It was expensive and drew funds away from other projects of PPLC. It did not generate the amount of publicity that had been expected; nor did it uncover a test case. A test case did not emerge until two years later, through the efforts of a dedicated physician named Charles Lee Buxton.

## DR. CHARLES LEE BUXTON:
## A "GENTLE CRUSADER"

Buxton was the recently appointed chair of Yale University's obstetrics and gynecology department. After graduating from Princeton University and Columbia University's medical school, he taught and practiced medicine, quite successfully, in New York City for some years. The position at Yale was Buxton's dream come true. When he was offered the post, he jumped at the chance, although it meant a substantial cut in his salary.

Buxton has been described as both research-minded and extremely compassionate. Soft-spoken but fierce in his resolve, Buxton was, according to Catherine Roraback, "devoted to his teaching, to research and to his students, and committed to his patients and their care."[7] He felt that the Connecticut birth control law interfered with his ability to deliver the quality of care his patients deserved. "The problem," Roraback remembers him saying "is that women who have private doctors can get all the information they want and get prescriptions [for birth control]. The real problem in Connecticut is that poor women who do not have private doctors cannot get that kind of care."[8]

Charles Lee Buxton was familiar with Planned Parenthood, partly because he ran the infertility clinic that it funded at Yale. Estelle Griswold had also recruited him to testify at the 1957 legislative session. Buxton had been shocked by what he had seen and heard there—"the atmosphere, the vituperation, the animus."[9] After carefully preparing and presenting the tragic stories of his patients who had suffered or died from pregnancies that could have been prevented, he listened to the outlandish and, Buxton thought, irresponsible claims that physicians for the other side were making.

*C. Lee Buxton, the physician who worked with Estelle Griswold to overturn the old Connecticut law that prohibited the use of contraceptives*

"Many women using contraceptive devices are frigid, and present a variety of ailments which are really a manifestation of their lack of sexual gratification," one stated. "Psychiatrists have noted that the problem child's behavior can be traced to the emotionally unstable and sexually frustrated mother using birth control measures," asserted another.[10] Buxton left the session convinced that the birth control law would not be overturned by lobbying the Connecticut legislature and more resolved than ever to change it.

### FORMULATING A TEST CASE

The series of cases that would eventually lead to *Griswold v. Connecticut* began at a cocktail party given by Estelle Griswold, when Charles Lee Buxton, known as Lee, met Fowler Harper, a gregarious Yale University law professor. Buxton spoke to Harper of his patients who needed birth control and his frustrations with the Connecticut law. Harper reacted with characteristic enthusiasm as he immediately saw the possibility of pressing a case arguing that the law was unconstitutional: it interfered with Buxton's right to practice medicine as he saw fit and with his patients' right to get the treatment they needed. Harper asked Buxton to find patients who would be willing to go forward as plaintiffs. Without delay, Buxton approached three patients and their husbands about the possibility of being involved in a test case.

One of these patients was Ruth O. Her husband Bob, a veteran of the Korean War, was working in a dairy company when Ruth became pregnant. Her pregnancy ended tragically: her blood pressure skyrocketed, she had a stroke, and the baby was stillborn at seven months. The stroke left Ruth with impaired speech, limited use of her right leg and arm, and crushed hopes. Moreover, Buxton felt sure, if Ruth were to become pregnant again, the strain on her system would kill her.

Another couple was Anne and Hector Kinloch. Anne was a secretary to the Episcopal chaplain of Yale University and her husband Hector was a doctoral candidate in Yale's history department. Anne had been through four miscarriages: two in a previous marriage and two with Hector. She had been traumatized by such devastating loss.

The third couple, Elizabeth and David O., had recently lost their third baby—just ten weeks old—to an incurable illness. Another pregnancy, and the very real possibility of another loss, would cause Elizabeth O. physical as well as emotional harm.

Harper came up with his own reasons for wanting to push the test case. In the fall of 1957, a student at the law school, Marvin Durning, had come to him complaining about the difficulty that he and his fiancée, Jean Cressey, a master's student in Yale's teaching program, had had getting birth control. Unable to acquire a prescription for birth control in the state of Connecticut, Jean was told that she would have to travel to a Planned Parenthood clinic in Westchester County, New York. Although Jean made the trip, which took an entire day, both she and Marvin were upset at the inconvenience of the Connecticut law. Harper was indignant when he heard their story.

Shortly after his conversation with Durning, Harper called Buxton. Buxton also had news to share. He told Harper about patients who might be appropriate test cases. Buxton then called Estelle Griswold to tell her that the test cases were becoming a real possibility, and she promptly scheduled a luncheon meeting at the New Haven Lawn Club in January.

Harper, who was not a member of the Connecticut Bar Association, realized that he would need to involve a lawyer who could argue the cases in the Connecticut courts. He expected the cases to go to the U.S. Supreme Court and planned to present the oral argument himself at that level. He called Catherine Roraback, a graduate of Mount Holyoke College and Yale Law School with a law practice in New Haven. She and Harper had met in Washington fifteen years earlier when she was working for the Agriculture Department and the National War Labor Board. He explained the case to her and invited her to the Lawn Club luncheon.

At the January meeting, Fowler Harper explained the case strategy to Buxton, Griswold, and Roraback. They would request a ruling called a "declaratory judgment" from the court stating that the 1879 statute was unconstitutional. They hoped, at the very least, to obtain a ruling that the statute should not apply in instances in which a woman's health or life would be threatened by a pregnancy. They did not expect to win in the Connecticut courts. The goal of the litigation would be to argue and win the case before the Supreme Court of the United States.

### THE STRATEGY
Fowler Harper intended to attack the statute from three angles. First, Dr. Buxton would argue that he should not be prevented from giving medical advice to his patients. After the Supreme Court's dismissal of the *Tileston* case on the grounds that a doctor could not bring a lawsuit to enforce the constitutional rights of his patients, it was decided that Buxton's patients would also file their own claims, stating that without birth control their lives and health would be threatened. Finally, the

Durnings would claim that *any* married couples, even physically healthy ones, should not be barred by the state from obtaining or using birth control. Roraback and Harper left that afternoon ready to begin work on the complaints—the documents that, when filed with a court, initiate a lawsuit.

By May 1958, Harper and Roraback had finished the five complaints, one for each of the plaintiffs. They were ready to be signed by Buxton and the four couples. Each couple had been assigned a pseudonym for the court action. (Fictional names were used because of the personal and painful nature of each case.) On the complaint, the Durnings became "Ralph and Rena Roe"; Ruth O. became "Jane Doe"; the Kinlochs, "Harold and Hannah Hoe"; and Elizabeth and David O., "Paul and Pauline Poe." The cases were filed on May 22, 1958.

While they waited for the state attorney general's office to respond to the claims, Loraine Campbell, the president of the Planned Parenthood Federation of America, decided to investigate Fowler Harper's reputation in the legal community. It must have been disconcerting for Campbell, a resident of Cambridge, Massachusetts, to hear the range of opinions from her friends at Harvard University's law school. Their comments ranged from a "tremendous fighter" of "enormous courage," to a "sleazy character" and a "soggy thinker."[11] Despite this uneven critique and some second thoughts by Campbell, Harper remained the lead attorney on the case.

On December 5, 1958, Judge Frank T. Healey of Connecticut Superior Court—the trial court—heard the first arguments in *Buxton* and its four companion cases. Ray Cannon from the Connecticut attorney general's office argued that the issues before the court had already been raised and decided in two earlier cases: *Nelson* and *Tileston*. He also claimed that the plaintiffs could not bring the cases under fictitious names.

Roraback's response to the arguments was straightforward. *Nelson* and *Tileston* did not apply because "these people have the right to be allowed to continue normal marital relations without being inhibited by the state."[12] She also told the judge that another superior court judge had assured her that the names would not present a problem in the case.

A month later, Judge Healey issued an opinion in favor of the state of Connecticut. Roraback immediately filed an appeal with the Connecticut Supreme Court of Errors. About the same time, the Durnings informed Harper that they were moving to the West Coast. Their case, *Roe v. Ullman*, would have to be withdrawn, but David and Louise Trubek, two recently married students at Yale Law School, agreed to participate in the litigation as the Durnings' successors. Roraback filed their complaint in May 1959.

### THE APPEAL IN STATE COURT

On October 7, 1959, Roraback and Cannon argued the appeal. Roraback did not expect to win. The goal of Harper and Roraback was to take the cases to the U.S. Supreme Court. What did they expect the ultimate result to be? Years after the case had been decided, Catherine Roraback remembered:

> *We who were involved at that point, had no realistic thought that we would achieve wide, sweeping constitutional condemnation of the basic statute. . . . In fact, we really felt at our most optimistic moments that by this litigation, we might persuade the courts to*

*read into the statute an exception for a very
limited but compelling group—those married women such as Jane Doe whose very
lives would be threatened by pregnancy.*[13]

On December 22, 1959, the Connecticut Supreme
Court issued an opinion unanimously supporting
the 1879 statute. The opinion, written by Chief Justice Raymond E. Baldwin, deferred to the legislature as it emphasized the importance of separation
of powers: "In our tripartite system of government,
the judiciary accords to the legislature the right to
determine in the first instance what is the nature
and extent of the danger to the public health, safety,
morals and welfare and what are the measures
best calculated to meet the threat." Referring to the
numerous reform bills that had been rejected by
the Connecticut legislature over the years, the Connecticut Supreme Court held: "Courts cannot write
legislation by judicial decree. This is particularly so
when the Legislature has refused to rewrite the ex-
isting legislation."

## ON TO THE U.S. SUPREME COURT

Harper immediately appealed the decision to the
U.S. Supreme Court. The first substantive document that Harper filed with the Court was a jurisdictional statement. It described the basis for the
appeal, that is, why the Court should hear it, and
summarized the arguments of each of the appellants.

The jurisdictional statement that Harper submitted to the Court for *Poe v. Ullman* seemed to be
written to appeal as much to the emotions of the
justices as to their analytical sense. He wrote forcefully about a subject that was not easily discussed:

the right of married couples to "privacy in their homes and, indeed, in the most private part thereof." The crux of Harper's argument was that married couples had a right to privacy in their bedrooms. "They want to be let alone in the bedroom. . . . These married persons contend that they have a constitutional right to marital intercourse in the privacy of their homes under medically approved conditions, and under circumstances mutually satisfactory to them. What right, it may be asked, is more fundamental or more sacred?"[14] Harper also submitted a jurisdictional statement for *Buxton v. Ullman*, which focused on the right and obligation of doctors to protect patients, but it did not have the same heartfelt tone of the *Poe v. Ullman* statement. The *Poe* and *Buxton* jurisdictional statements came up for consideration before the Supreme Court six weeks after they were submitted.

The U.S. Supreme Court does not hear every case that is submitted to it on appeal. Each term, the justices vote to determine which cases of the many that are submitted they will hear. On May 20, 1960, at the closed-door meeting of the nine justices, five members of the Court—Chief Justice Earl Warren and Associate Justices William O. Douglas, John M. Harlan, William J. Brennan, Jr., and Potter Stewart—voted in favor of hearing *Buxton* and *Poe*. Justices Hugo L. Black, Tom C. Clark, and Charles E. Whittaker voted against hearing the appeal, and one justice, Felix Frankfurter, abstained from the vote. Frankfurter, as it turned out, later authored the opinion.

The time allotted for oral argument was, by Supreme Court standards, considerable. Each side would have ninety minutes to present its position.

In just one and one-half hours, Harper would have to argue in favor of changing a law that had resisted attempts by many skilled, powerful, and determined people for eighty years.

In September 1960, Harper submitted his brief, the written presentation of the facts of the case, the issues of law, and his arguments for changing the law. His brief sounded similar in some ways to the jurisdictional statement. The Connecticut statute, he argued, invaded "the privacy of the citizen" and regulated "the private sex life of all married people." He again emphasized that "these spouses want to be let alone in the bedroom" and that they have "a constitutionally protected right to marital intercourse in the privacy of their homes." His final words to the Court were that the Connecticut statute "interfere[d] mercilessly with the most intimate and sacred experiences in life."[15] Amicus curiae ("friend of the court") briefs, which are written by supporters with an interest in the case, were submitted by the American and Connecticut Civil Liberties Unions and the Planned Parenthood Federation of America.

To prepare for a hearing, Supreme Court justices commonly ask their law clerks to write memoranda analyzing the legal issues in the case. One of the clerks, Charles Fried, criticized Harper's brief sharply: "His jurisdictional statement is execrable and so is his brief on the merits—it misses the whole point that can be made for his position."[16] Fried agreed, however, with Harper's position that there was a constitutionally protected right to privacy that applied to intimacy between married couples in their homes. According to Fried, the chief problem with *Poe* was that since it was highly unlikely that the law would ever be enforced, litigation to overturn the law was unnecessary. As for *Buxton,* Fried noted that there was no right for physicians to practice without any regulation by the state. In fact, the state already regulated physicians in many areas of their practice.

## THE ARGUMENTS BEFORE THE COURT

At 2:45 P.M., on Wednesday March 1, 1961, *Poe* and *Buxton* were called to be heard before the bench; all nine justices were present. Fowler Harper presented his arguments to the justices first.

Harper began by describing the medical situations of the plaintiffs. His argument was interrupted by the justices on several occasions as they asked questions about the law and the case. Did the Connecticut law prohibit the sale or prescription of contraception? Was Harper challenging the law as it applied to all people or only as it applied to women whose health was seriously threatened? Why hadn't Harper argued that the law had violated Dr. Buxton's right to free speech? Was freedom of religion involved in this case? Near the end of his argument, Harper was asked about the enforcement of the statutes: How many prosecutions a year were there in Connecticut under the statutes? Is the law really enforced?

At about 4:00 P.M., it was Ray Cannon's turn to present his argument to the members of the Court. He, too, was questioned by the justices after several minutes of his rambling presentation. Chief Justice Warren went first: Could Connecticut deny lifesaving treatment to someone like Jane Doe? Cannon's response, that "it is the problem primarily for the legislature to determine what is the greater good and how to accomplish the greater good," drew a sarcastic response from Potter Stewart. He remarked that Cannon's response was like "telling a patient that they had appendicitis and would die unless it was removed, but that appendix removals were not allowed." Cannon was also asked: Was there an "outside authoritarian power" influencing the Connecticut legislature? Did Cannon personally regard the sale of certain items for the prevention of disease to be legal in Connecticut? Cannon responded no to both questions.

Echoing law clerk Charles Fried's concerns about whether enforcement of the statute was a real fear, Felix Frankfurter mused, "We're talking about a theoretical thing here, aren't we?"[17]

Fowler Harper returned, finally, to respond to Cannon's statements. When he noted that contraception was available in pharmacies in Connecticut, one of the justices noted that "this may all be an abstract attack on the law." Realizing, perhaps, what he had said, Harper asserted that the law did have an effect and that under the law clinics could not operate. As time ran out, however, Justice Brennan commented, "I take it that the Poes and Does can get what they need almost anyplace in Connecticut."[18]

For roughly three months, Harper and Griswold and others involved waited for the Court's opinion in *Poe* and *Buxton*. During the wait, Estelle Griswold considered what PPLC should do next and resolved to open a clinic. If the law were struck down, PPLC wanted to offer birth control services immediately. If the law remained in place, Griswold wanted to test its limits. Harper told a gathering of PPLC supporters that if the Supreme Court ruled against them, the next step would be to have Estelle Griswold thrown in jail.

## THE SUPREME COURT'S RESPONSE

On June 19, 1961, the Supreme Court handed down a decision dismissing the appeals in *Doe, Poe,* and *Buxton.* Justice Felix Frankfurter wrote the decision, in which he was joined by three other justices. Four justices filed dissenting opinions and one justice submitted a concurring opinion. (A concurring opinion agrees with the result of the majority opinion but offers different reasons for reaching that result; a dissenting opinion disagrees with the main opinion of a court.)

Frankfurter wrote that it was not clear that the state had threatened to prosecute either the patients—the Does and the Poes—or Dr. Buxton. He pointed out that, indeed, except for *Nelson,* there had been no prosecutions under the law since it was enacted in 1879. There are many requirements that a case must meet before it can be decided by the U.S. Supreme Court. One of these requirements is that an actual controversy must be presented to the Court. With no threat of prosecution under the law, Frankfurter found no controversy. Therefore, there was no constitutional issue to decide. In the passage that contains the most well-remembered words of the case, he wrote:

> *The fact that Connecticut has not chosen to press the enforcement of this statute deprives these controversies of the immediacy which is an indispensable condition of constitutional adjudication. This Court cannot be umpire to debates concerning harmless, empty shadows. To find it necessary to pass on these statutes now, in order to protect appellants from the hazards of prosecution, would be to close our eyes to reality.*[19]

*Felix Frankfurter, the Supreme Court
justice who wrote the 1961 opinions
for* Doe, Poe, *and* Buxton

Justice William J. Brennan wrote a concurring opinion that practically invited another lawsuit. Stating that he agreed with the result in this case he nonetheless conceded that there was an actual controversy brewing in Connecticut. The controversy was not whether the law prevented married couples from using birth control, but whether the law prevented birth control clinics from operating. Brennan put it this way:

> *The true controversy in this case is over the opening of birth-control clinics on a large scale; it is that which the State has prevented in the past, not the use of contraceptives by isolated and individual married couples. It will be time enough to decide the constitutional question urged upon us when, if ever, that real controversy flares up again.*[20]

The dissenting opinion authored by Justice William O. Douglas expressed particular frustration with Frankfurter's opinion. Douglas had a long-standing feud with Frankfurter, and he would later write the *Griswold* opinion. His sentiments were evident in his dissent:

> *What are these people—doctor and patients—to do? Flout the law and go to prison? Violate the law surreptitiously and hope they will not get caught? By today's decision we leave them no other alternatives. . . . A sick wife, a concerned husband, a conscientious doctor seek a dignified, discrete, orderly answer to the critical problem confronting them. We should not turn them away and make them flout the law and get*

*arrested to have their constitutional rights determined. . . . They are entitled to an answer to their predicament here and now.*[21]

Justice John M. Harlan wrote a lengthy dissent that remains perhaps the most important part of the decision. Clearly opposed to the statute as it applied to married couples, Harlan wrote a description of the right of privacy that would resurface later in the *Griswold v. Connecticut* decision. In his view, marriage was an institution protected from unreasonable intrusion by the due process clause of the Fourteenth Amendment. Harlan considered the statute unreasonable, as well as "obnoxiously intrusive." "The intimacy of husband and wife is necessarily an essential and accepted feature of the institution of marriage, an institution which the State not only must allow, but which always and in every age it has fostered and protected." He also foreshadowed the cases that would follow *Griswold* when he asserted that the right of privacy is "not an absolute." He continued, "Thus, I would not suggest that adultery, homosexuality, fornication and incest are immune from criminal enquiry."[22]

A final, ironic coda to the *Poe* decision can be found in the pages of a Connecticut newspaper, the *Wallingford Post*. On March 3, 1961, the U.S. Supreme Court voted privately to dismiss the case because it was unlikely that the antiquated statute would ever be enforced. No doubt, such reasoning would have interested Thomas Coccomo, a forty-year-old salesman who, on that same day, was arrested in Connecticut for peddling condoms to gas station owners. North Haven police found nearly one hundred dollars' worth of contraception in his car and charged him under the aiding and abetting section of the statute. During the weeks that Supreme Court clerks and justices drafted the opinion in *Poe*, Coccomo appeared in Wallingford Circuit Court, where he was convicted and fined seventy-five dollars.

# Chapter 5

# CLIMBING BACK TO THE SUPREME COURT

Estelle Griswold's response to the *Poe* decision was swift. On June 20, 1961, the day after *Poe* was announced, she told reporters that since the law had been declared a "dead duck," PPLC would open a birth control clinic in New Haven in September. What if the authorities chose to fight the opening of a clinic? "We would of course welcome prosecution by the state."[1] More and more, it seemed that the only approach that would succeed in repealing the 1879 law was direct confrontation with the authorities.

The Planned Parenthood Federation of America (PPFA) supported the plan to offer clinic services in Connecticut. It issued a statement to the press welcoming "the recognition by the Court that the law has in fact become a nullity" and confirming that PPLC would open a public clinic "as rapidly as possible."[2]

By July, Griswold signed a lease at 79 Trumbull

Street on behalf of PPLC. The organization rented nine rooms one block from its old office and, coincidentally, in the same mansion that the Connecticut Birth Control League had used as its headquarters some thirty years previously. Griswold announced that she hoped to open the clinic on October 1. Its services were certainly welcome; calls for appointments came in at the rate of ten to fifteen each week.

Although she did not meet her October 1 deadline, it was not due to lack of effort. Estelle Griswold was not afraid to roll up her sleeves. To prepare the clinic, she "scrounged around for furniture . . . [and] scrubbed its floors to make it a 'warm and hospitable place where married women would feel comfortable.' "[3] Lee Buxton also worked to secure donations of equipment for the clinic from a local hospital.

The clinic was to operate three days a week in two-hour sessions. Under executive director Estelle Griswold and medical director Lee Buxton, volunteer staff and four doctors contributed their time and services. Unmarried women would not be accepted as patients unless they were referred by members of the clergy for premarital fittings of diaphragms.

Griswold scheduled the first ten appointments for the evening of November 1; then she announced a press conference for the following day. She was blunt about her strategy in opening the clinic. "It is our hope that someone will complain and that the State Attorney in New Haven will act to close the center. We shall then carry our case to the U.S. Supreme Court and this time we feel they shall have to make a decision."[4]

Griswold, Harper, Buxton, and PPLC president Lucia Parks faced about forty reporters that Thurs-

ANNOUNCE NEW CLINIC—The Planned Parenthood League of Connecticut formally announced at a news conference yesterday the opening of a trial birth control clinic at 79 Trumbull St. Left to right are league members Dr. Charles B. Cheney, a member of the clinic's medical advisory board; Mrs. Charles H. Parks, president of the state league; Dr. C. Lee Buxton, medical director of the clinic, and Fowler Harper, counsel for the league.

# Birth Control Clinic Opens Here; Sponsors Defy Connecticut Law

*Local newspapers covered the press conference attended by (from left to right) League officials Charles Cheney, Lucia Parks, C. Lee Buxton, and Fowler Harper.*

day morning. They described their operating schedule—Tuesday mornings, Wednesday evenings, and Friday afternoons—as well as the enthusiastic response they had received from women interested in obtaining contraceptive services. They also told reporters about their successful start-up the previous evening. Buxton talked a bit about his patients, the women whose situations had moved him so greatly. Harper spoke openly about their intent: "I think it would be a state and community service if a criminal action were brought. I think citizens and doctors alike are entitled to know if they are violating the law."[5]

James Morris, the night manager at the local car rental agency, would inadvertently do his part to fulfill Harper's wish by notifying the police of the clinic's activities. After detectives John Blazi and Harold Berg visited the clinic to confirm its activities, Julius Maretz, the circuit court prosecutor, was ready to make a deal with Griswold.

In a cooperative gesture of respect for the privacy of the clinic's patients, Maretz sent Berg and Blazi back to the clinic with an offer for Griswold. If she would provide the names of two women who would admit that they had received contraceptives and counseling at the center, he would not attempt to confiscate other medical records. Griswold said she would call the detectives later in the day with the names.

Griswold could come up with only one name: Joan Bates Forsberg. Forsberg, a graduate of the Yale Divinity School, was a thirty-three-year-old mother of three. Her husband, also a pastor, worked in an inner-city parish. Before the New Haven clinic opened, Forsberg had gone to a Planned Parenthood clinic across the state border in New York. Griswold remembered that Forsberg had gratefully offered to help in any way when she paid her two-dollar fee for a supply of birth control pills. Now, Forsberg agreed to make a statement to Detective Blazi with the understanding that the case would be against Griswold and Buxton, not herself.

As for the second client, Griswold was stuck. She needed a patient who had seen Buxton, but she was unable to find anyone suitable for the case. She told Harper of her problem and he volunteered to find her another patient. He turned to the wife of a young member of the Yale Law School faculty. Rosemary Stevens, an Englishwoman and student at the Yale School of Public Health, agreed to meet Buxton at the clinic and make a statement to the police that she had visited the clinic and received a supply of contraceptives.

On November 10, 1961, arrest warrants were issued for Griswold and Buxton. In keeping with the courteous tone that had been established, Maretz called Catherine Roraback to ask her to have her clients surrender at the detectives' office.

After the arrest proceedings of Griswold and Buxton, during which they made no statement to the police, the two told the press of their disappointment that the clinic could not serve its patients. Griswold described a letter that PPLC would send to women whose appointments had been canceled. The letter would include information about seven types of birth control that were easily available in Connecticut and addresses and phone numbers of clinics in neighboring states.

On November 15 and 16, a seemingly small, but critical, loose end was tied up. Rosemary Stevens and Joan Forsberg arrived at the detectives' office to state that they had received contraceptives from the clinic and that they had in fact *used* them. This was in accordance with the charges, which stated that the women who were furnished contraceptives "did in fact use said drugs, medicinal articles, and instruments for the purpose of preventing conception." The detectives confiscated both Stevens's "partially used tube of vaginal jelly" and Forsberg's remaining supply of birth control pills. Forsberg went home and immediately called Griswold to ask for a new supply. "I said I don't mind going to jail for this cause," Forsberg told her, "but getting pregnant is another story."[6]

Meanwhile, James Morris continued his campaign, sending registered letters to Connecticut officials, including the governor, and finally, dictating a complaint to Detective Berg. "I filed this complaint to protect my children and all children and people against juvenile and adult delinquency," Morris said, angry that anyone could walk into the PPLC clinic and walk out with their "immoral literature." Mostly, it seems, Morris was distressed that PPLC's opening of the clinic caused "many innocent people to break the law of this state." When Berg asked Morris what his reaction would be if the birth control statute was repealed, Morris answered, "I would say that they had a right then to operate."[7]

## BACK TO THE COURTS

Once again, the birth control advocates faced a long, slow climb to the U.S. Supreme Court. At one point along the way, Buxton, frustrated by the long waiting periods between arguments and judicial decisions, remarked: "If the medical profession were as desultory as lawyers, most of our cases would be dead by this time."[8]

The strategy would be the same as in *Poe*. There was no expectation of winning in the state courts of Connecticut; the goal was to get to the

U.S. Supreme Court. Griswold emphasized this point several times along the way. Even as they lost each hearing and appeal in the Connecticut courts, Griswold was confident of a victory in the Supreme Court.

At a hearing held in November 1961, Griswold and Buxton pleaded not guilty to violating the statute. At the next hearing, on December 8, both sides presented their oral arguments to Judge Lacey. Roraback stated the essence of their claim: "The married person in the privacy of his own home has a right to engage in marital relations and to do so in such a manner as he sees fit—he and she, forgive me, see fit. To hold otherwise would invade the very innermost sanctums of privacy in violation of the rights of individuals to privacy which are embodied in the term 'liberty' in the Fourteenth Amendment."[9] Maretz's argument was straightforward: the law required him to prosecute all violations of the statute. Lacey said that he would take the matter under advisement and issue a ruling after considering the arguments of both sides.

## THE TRIAL

On December 22, Judge Lacey filed a short decision and set a trial date of January 2, 1962. There was no jury at the trial, but the crowd numbered about 100 people. The prosecution put on their witnesses first. Detectives Berg and Blazi testified to their conversations with Estelle Griswold. Joan Forsberg and Rosemary Stevens then were called to testify that they had in fact received birth control devices from the clinic.

Estelle Griswold was the first witness for the defense. Under Roraback's direction, she detailed

*Clinic directors Estelle Griswold (center) and C. Lee Buxton (right) talk with their attorney, Catherine Roraback, during their trial testing Connecticut's eighty-two-year-old birth control law.*

the work of the PPLC clinic. Alluding to *Poe*, she stated, "If the Supreme Court had declared this law a nullity, a dead word and a harmless empty shadow, I do not see how I could commit an offense against such a law."[10] Buxton also testified. At the end of Buxton's testimony, James Morris again entered the fray, offering his opinion from the spectator's section. Judge Lacey had the bailiff remove him from the courtroom. Directly after the closing remarks, Judge Lacey found both defendants guilty and fined them each $100.

Roraback appealed the decision to the Appellate Division of the Connecticut Circuit Court, which unanimously affirmed the convictions of Griswold and Buxton. An unexpected statement by the Catholic Church boosted the spirits of birth control supporters in the spring of 1963. PPLC was considering yet another effort to repeal the statute in the legislature when Boston archbishop Richard Cardinal Cushing made the shocking announcement during a radio broadcast that the Catholic Church had changed its position on birth control statutes. It no longer supported them. "Even in that field," Cushing said, "I have no right to impose my thinking, which is rooted in religious thought, on those who do not think as I do." At the legislative hearing that spring, "the room—filled mostly with women—gasped and then broke into applause when a call for opponents brought no one to his feet."[11]

Meanwhile, Estelle Griswold was facing controversy within the ranks of PPLC. Her nine-and-a-half-year tenure as executive director of PPLC was nearly brought to an abrupt end when she submitted her formal resignation on April 17, 1963. The trouble centered around a house that PPLC had purchased for renovation near the 79 Trumbull

Street building. Griswold wanted to buy the carriage house that sat behind the building to serve as her residence. She thought the arrangement would make it easier to cope with her husband's emphysema, caused by years of cigarette smoking. He could barely climb the stairs at their house at 40 Trumbull Street. Other PPLC members objected to the deal. It is possible that objections were more personal than ethical or financial. Complaints about Estelle took a personal tone: "super-aggressive," "sometimes a bit maddening," and "something of a snob" were some of the descriptions Estelle's closest friends used for her.[12] These personal attacks prompted her resignation.

PPLC's top officers agreed immediately that Griswold had to withdraw her resignation. At a May 2 meeting, the board refused her resignation, apologized for conveying anything but its full confidence in her, and praised her leadership ability. Griswold withdrew her resignation and left the meeting victorious. Not only was the carriage house deal intact, but she also was authorized to use PPLC's car for personal business.

### BEFORE THE HIGHEST COURT IN CONNECTICUT

Finally, in November 1963, the argument in *Griswold* was to be heard by the Connecticut appeals court. From there, the next step would be the U.S. Supreme Court.

The argument went well enough for Roraback. In fact, the judge, Chief Justice John H. King, seemed to be tougher on the prosecutor, Joe Clark, than he was on her. He asked Clark some pointed, very difficult questions: "Does this law really protect morality? How are you going to know if someone uses contraceptives unless they tell you? I

**91**

assume you are not going to raid bedrooms? Would it be reasonable to abolish all liquor to prevent drunken driving?"[13]

Despite Roraback's skillful work both on paper and at the hearing, no one at Planned Parenthood expected the Connecticut Supreme Court to overturn the lower court's decision.

While the decision was pending, Estelle Griswold endured a trial of another sort; her husband went through major surgery for ever-worsening emphysema. And Fowler Harper was also ill, with prostate cancer.

The opinion from the Connecticut court came down in May 1964. Not surprisingly, the court unanimously affirmed the decision of the lower court in a short decision that cited *Nelson*, *Tileston*, and *Poe* as precedents. Roraback and Harper were already working on the appeal to the U.S. Supreme Court.

### BEFORE THE U.S. SUPREME COURT

Harper submitted the appeal and the jurisdictional statement to the Supreme Court in September 1964. His argument emphasized that Griswold and Buxton had been deprived of liberty and property rights guaranteed by the First and the Fourteenth Amendments. He argued that the law deprived Dr. Buxton of his right to advise his patients. That right, he claimed, was protected by the First Amendment right to free speech. In addition, by prohibiting Dr. Buxton from advising his patients as he saw fit, the law interfered with his right to make a living, thus depriving him of an important property right without due process of law. The law forbidding the use of contraceptives, he argued, deprived his married patients of liberty and privacy rights.

With tensions around the case running high, all the parties were busy that fall as they waited for the Court's decision. Would the justices vote to hear the appeal? Assistant prosecutor Joe Clark filed a motion asking that the case be dismissed partly on the grounds that the Court had already refused to hear a case involving the same issues some twenty-six years earlier.

Estelle Griswold and Lee Buxton continued to struggle with the leadership of PPLC. At one point, both Griswold and Buxton resigned and then, after concessions were made, withdrew their resignations.

Meanwhile, Fowler Harper and Catherine Roraback battled members of PPFA. PPFA executives were highly critical of the papers Harper had submitted to the Supreme Court in the *Griswold* appeal and angry that he had filed a response to Joe Clark's motion to dismiss without consulting them.

On December 7, the Supreme Court announced that it had voted unanimously to hear the *Griswold* appeal. It was a milestone in the case; yet it was nearly overshadowed by the tragic news that Fowler Harper was losing his long fight against cancer. On December 8, he entered the hospital for the last time and died one month later.

*Thomas Emerson, the attorney and professor who took over the Griswold case after Fowler Harper's death*

# Chapter 6

# A DECISION AT LAST

**B**efore his death, Fowler Harper had talked with Thomas Emerson, a friend and fellow member of the Yale Law School faculty, to see if Emerson would take his place on the case. Emerson and Harper shared similar political views, but they had very different personalities. Harper was flamboyant and dramatic, while Emerson was quiet and reserved. Emerson consented to take the case and started to work on the brief, which was due in early February.

On February 11, 1965, Emerson filed a ninety-six-page brief. In it, he argued that the Connecticut law violated the appellants' rights to liberty under the Fourteenth Amendment to the Constitution and that it also violated Buxton's and Griswold's right to freedom of speech under the First Amendment. He also identified a right of privacy, the boundaries of which, he wrote, "have not yet been spelled out," but which "plainly . . . extend to un-warranted government invasion of (1) the sanctity of the home, and (2) the intimacies of the sexual relationship in marriage." The precise source of the right of privacy was also uncertain, but Emerson was clear that that did not dilute the power of the right: "Whether one derives the right of privacy from a composite of the Third, Fourth and Fifth Amendments, from the Ninth Amendment, or from the 'liberty' clause of the Fourteenth Amendment, such a constitutional right has been specifically recognized in this Court."[1]

By comparison, Joe Clark, the attorney for the state of Connecticut, submitted a much shorter brief, only thirty-four pages long, arguing that there had been no invasion of anyone's right of privacy. Oral arguments were scheduled for March 29, 1965.

### BEFORE THE JUSTICES

At 1:30 P.M. on March 29, Catherine Roraback and Thomas Emerson sat at counsel table in front of the nine justices of the Supreme Court. Estelle Griswold; Fowler's widow, Miriam; and Emerson's wife, Ruth, were seated behind the bar in the filled courtroom.

Emerson was the first to speak. He presented his argument, interrupted frequently by tough questions from the justices, for nearly an hour. The justices probed the rationale behind Emerson's arguments: what constitutional provisions supported his theories? Emerson cited the Ninth Amendment "as a basis for the right of privacy," as well as the "Third, Fourth and Fifth Amendments, insofar as they embody a concept of a right of privacy." On the right of privacy, Emerson opined, "If there's any right that you would think would be reserved to the people and which the government should not interfere with, it would be this right."[2] Emerson's argument stopped just before 2:30 P.M.

Before the Court adjourned for the day, Joe Clark spoke for the state of Connecticut for just a few minutes. He admitted that he thought the law was "foolish," but not unconstitutional. "Legislatures have the right to enact stupid laws," he told the Court.[3] The following day at 10:00 A.M., they reconvened. In response to questions from the justices, Clark explained that the purpose of the statute was to protect morality. The right of privacy was not involved, he stated, because the clinic was public and open to the world. He also argued that married couples did not have the right to do whatever they wanted concerning contraception and that the states had the right to regulate birth control clinics.

The oral argument closed with a ten-minute rebuttal by Emerson that ended with a glimpse of things to come. Justice Black asked, "Would your argument concerning these things you've been talking about relating to privacy, invalidate all laws that punish people for bringing about abortions?" Emerson, understandably unable to predict the future of American jurisprudence answered, "No, I think it would not cover the abortion laws . . . that conduct does not occur in the privacy of the home."[4] Of course, *Roe v. Wade*, the well-known 1973 case that made abortion legal, would prove him wrong.

### THE DECISION

Three days later, the nine Supreme Court justices met privately to discuss the case. At the end of the

*The attorney for the state of Connecticut, Joe Clark (center), speaks with the prosecutor who investigated the clinic, Julius Maretz (right), and another attorney on the steps of the Supreme Court Building in Washington, D.C., before participating in the argument before the high court.*

meeting, seven justices voted to overturn the convictions of Griswold and Buxton and two justices voted to affirm the decision of the lower court.

The two dissenters from the majority were Justices Potter Stewart and Hugo L. Black. Stewart's reasoning for upholding the statute was that he could not find anything in the Constitution that prohibited Connecticut from having such a law on the books. Therefore, it was the job of the Connecticut legislature, and not the Supreme Court, to repeal the law, if it chose to do so. Nor could Black find a reason to reverse. On the First Amendment argument, Black was even sarcastic. The First Amendment, he said, meant "the right of assembly, and the right of husband and wife to assemble in bed is a new right of assembly to me."⁵

The job of drafting the opinion was assigned by Chief Justice Earl Warren to William O. Douglas. Justice Douglas was, to put it mildly, a controversial figure on the Supreme Court. Although he was widely regarded as one of the most intelligent justices, his hastily drafted opinions could be disappointing. There were those who thought he was lazy and sloppy.

Justice Douglas had written a first draft of the opinion quickly. It was then circulated to Justice Brennan who, helped by his law clerk, suggested some sweeping revisions. The final draft was greatly improved as a result. Douglas issued the opinion on June 7, 1965. It was short, slightly more than six pages long, and it declared the Connecticut law unconstitutional.

Douglas began by discussing the Supreme Court's authority to overrule a law enacted by a state legislature. (Out of respect for each state's right to conduct its business as it sees fit, the Court is usually reluctant to strike down a state law. It will not do so unless there is a compelling reason.)

*Justice William O. Douglas wrote the* Griswold *opinion that declared the old Connecticut law unconstitutional in 1965.*

Douglas confirmed that the Court does not "sit as a super-legislature" passing judgment on state laws concerning economics, business, or social policy. The issues in *Griswold* were different, however. The case involved "an intimate relation of husband and wife and their physician's role in one aspect of that relation."[6]

He then explained that marital relations were basic rights protected by the Constitution, even though the Constitution did not mention this right. The right was not the only unmentioned, or unenumerated, right protected by the Constitution. Douglas used the First Amendment as an example. The First Amendment had been interpreted by the Court to protect unenumerated rights such as the "association of people," "the right to educate a child in a school of the parents' choice," and "the right to study any particular subject or any foreign language." Douglas called these "peripheral rights." And he asserted that another peripheral right protected by the First Amendment is the right of privacy. "The First Amendment," Douglas wrote, "has a penumbra"—a region surrounding the core— "where privacy is protected from governmental intrusion."[7]

Other amendments besides the First Amendment also protected the right of privacy as a peripheral right. Douglas's now famous flowery rhetoric expressing this idea has amused and confounded law students and lawyers since he first wrote: "Specific guarantees in the Bill of Rights have penumbras, formed by emanations from those guarantees that help give them life and substance. . . . Various guarantees create zones of privacy." This case, he continued, "concerns a relationship lying within the zone of privacy created by several fundamental constitutional guarantees."[8]

Having explained the source of the right of privacy, Justice Douglas concluded his opinion with an impassioned plea:

> *Would we allow the police to search the sacred precincts of marital bedrooms for telltale signs of the use of contraceptives? The very idea is repulsive to the notions of privacy surrounding the marriage relationship.*
>
> *We deal with a right of privacy older than the Bill of Rights—older than our political parties, older than our school system. Marriage is a coming together for better or worse, hopefully enduring, and intimate to the degree of being sacred. . . . It is an association for as noble a purpose as any involved in our prior decisions.*[9]

## CONCURRING AND DISSENTING OPINIONS

Three concurring opinions accompanied the Douglas opinion. Twice as long as the Douglas opinion, the first concurrence came from the chambers of Justice Arthur J. Goldberg and was joined by those of Chief Justice Earl Warren and Justice William J. Brennan, Jr. Goldberg's clerk, a young man named Stephen Breyer, researched and wrote the first draft of this concurrence. In July 1994, that former clerk was confirmed as the 108th justice of the Supreme Court, appointed by President Bill Clinton.

Justice Goldberg's concurrence asserted that the "concept of liberty" protects some fundamental rights, including the right of privacy in marriage, that are not enumerated in the Bill of Rights. To support this theory, he relied on the Ninth Amendment. (Justice Douglas had also referred to the Ninth Amendment but without elaboration.) Rarely used, this part of the Bill of Rights states "the enumeration in the Constitution, of certain rights, shall not be construed to deny or disparage others retained by the people." Goldberg used the Ninth Amendment to demonstrate that the framers of the Constitution believed that there were unenumerated fundamental rights that exist as surely as those rights which are specifically mentioned. He phrased it this way:

> *Although the Constitution does not speak in so many words of the right of privacy in marriage, I cannot believe that it offers these fundamental rights no protection. The fact that no particular provision of the Constitution explicitly forbids the State from disrupting the traditional relation of the family—a relation as old and as fundamental as our entire civilization—surely does not show that the Government was meant to have the power to do so. Rather as the Ninth Amendment expressly recognizes, there are fundamental personal rights such as this one, which are protected from abridgment by the Government though not specifically mentioned in the Constitution.*[10]

The second concurring opinion was written by Justice Harlan, author of the important dissenting opinion in *Poe*. Harlan did not need to look to the Bill of Rights or any of its "emanations." He believed that sufficient rationale for overturning the statute could be found in the due process clause of the Fourteenth Amendment which, in his view, protected a concept of liberty that was larger than the specific rights listed in the Constitution. "The Due Process Clause of the Fourteenth Amendment," he asserted, "stands, in my opinion, on its own bottom."[11]

Justice Byron R. "Whizzer" White, a former college football star, wrote the third concurrence. He emphasized that the state's purpose for enacting the law—to discourage illicit sexual relations—was insufficient to justify the scope of the statute. In his opinion, the statute deprived married people of liberty without due process of law.

Both of the dissenters, Justices Black and Stewart, acknowledged that they found the law to be detestable, but could not find justification for overturning it. Justice Black wrote a dissent to the Douglas opinion in which he expressed one of the more common criticisms of the *Griswold* opinion:

> *The Court talks about a constitutional "right of privacy" as though there is some constitutional provision or provisions forbidding any law ever to be passed which might abridge the "privacy" of individuals. But there is not. . . .*

> *. . . I like my privacy as well as the next one, but I am nevertheless compelled to admit that government has a right to invade it unless prohibited by some specific constitutional provision.*[12]

Justice Potter Stewart wrote in a separate dissent that the Connecticut statute was an "uncommonly silly law," although like Black, he found no violation of the Constitution. "I believe," he continued, "the use of contraceptives in the relationship of

*The two dissenters in* Griswold v. Connecticut*:*
*Hugo L. Black and Potter Stewart*

marriage should be left to personal and private choice" and that "professional counsel about methods of birth control should be available to all."[13] However, neither could he find a constitutional provision to support the result he believed in. It was up to the people of Connecticut, he concluded, to repeal the law.

## REACTIONS TO *GRISWOLD*

The press's reactions to the decision were positive. The *New York Times* hailed the decision as a "milestone," and focused sharp criticism on the dissenters as well. Referring to the opinions espoused by Black and Stewart, a *Times* editorial asked: "A reasonable and convincing argument can be made . . . that this infringement on personal freedom . . . should have been corrected by the legislatures. But the fact is that it was not corrected. To what forum but the Supreme Court could the people then repair, after years of frustration, for relief from bigotry and enslavement?"[14]

The biggest supporter of the Connecticut law, the Catholic Church, accepted the decision without fiery criticism. But a spokesperson affirmed that Church teachings still prohibited contraception. "This is a judicial opinion, and it in no way involves the morality of the question," the Hartford archbishop told the press; "artificial contraception remains immoral by the law of God."[15]

The parties to the case had subdued reactions. They were, no doubt, pleased, but not surprised. They had expected to win. The victory was certainly muted by the fact that Fowler Harper was not there to share it. Miriam Harper, Fowler's widow, wrote to Justice Douglas to express her appreciation:

*The day after the Supreme Court handed down
its* Griswold *opinion, Estelle Griswold (left)
celebrated the win with a colleague in the
New Haven clinic where the case originated.*

*Having lived with Fowler through almost
every facet of the Birth Control case for the
past many years, I cannot refrain from writing to tell you how pleased Fowler would
have been with your opinion this week. It is
one of the great sadnesses of life that he
could not see his work come to fruition. . . . I
feel the outcome of this case is a fitting
memorial to Fowler and will have wide-
spread effects.*[16]

Lee Buxton flew to France soon after the decision
was announced, but not without first calling
Thomas Emerson from the airport to offer congrat-
ulations. As Emerson remembers it, Buxton joked
that in light of the success with *Griswold* they
should take on the laws prohibiting abortion next.
However, a few months later, Buxton was over-
whelmed by a combination of depression and alco-
holism. Forced to take a leave from Yale, within
months he was admitted to a psychiatric ward. He
did return to Yale briefly, but died a few years later.

Margaret Sanger, though old and frail, lived
long enough to see birth control made legal in Connecticut. She died just over a year later, on September 6, 1966.

On September 20, 1965, nine patients were present for the opening of the Planned Parenthood
League of Connecticut's clinic at 406 Orange Street
in New Haven. It was twenty-five years and six
months to the day since Sallie Pease had closed the
clinic in response to the decision in *State v. Nelson*.
After the successful opening of the clinic, Estelle
Griswold submitted her resignation to PPLC. This
time, nearly eleven years after she had first accepted the position as executive director, the League accepted her resignation without argument, though it

*In 1965, C. Lee Buxton and Estelle Griswold were honored by Planned Parenthood for their work to legalize birth control in Connecticut.*

did ask her to stay on while it searched for her successor. In recognition of her service, the Planned Parenthood Federation of America honored her, along with Lee Buxton, with its highest award.

For Estelle Griswold, Lee Buxton, and the many others who had worked long and hard to legalize birth control for married couples, the fight was over. The constitutional right to privacy, however, was in its infancy. New players would quickly emerge to test its limits.

# Chapter 7

# GRISWOLD AND AFTER

*Griswold v. Connecticut*, which finally felled the old Connecticut law, is a historic case that altered American constitutional history. Its effects on society and as a legal precedent can be viewed through many lenses.

Viewed narrowly, *Griswold* is the case that permitted married citizens to use contraception to control the growth of their families. Although this is not considered the most meaningful aspect of the case today, for those who lived in Connecticut before 1965 and fought for reproductive freedom, it was no small matter.

*Griswold* is also remembered as the case that created a constitutional right of privacy. Because *Roe v. Wade*, the case that later legalized abortion, relied on the right of privacy and because this right is not mentioned in the Constitution, *Griswold v. Connecticut* still generates active controversy.

As recently as 1987, one U.S. Supreme Court

nominee, Judge Robert Bork, saw his nomination fail largely because he questioned the validity of the right first announced in *Griswold*. Bork called *Griswold* a "radical departure" and explained that it "established . . . a privacy right on reasoning which was utterly inadequate, and failed to define that right so we know what it applies to." Since the Bork hearings, *Griswold* has been called "the Senate's litmus test for federal judges."[1]

Other legal scholars agree with Judge Bork, questioning whether there is a constitutional right of privacy, as outlined in *Griswold*. While conceding that the notion of a right of privacy in our personal affairs is appealing, they ask: if the framers of the Constitution had meant for there to be a right of privacy, why didn't they write it into the document?

For those legal theorists who support the idea that we hold some fundamental rights that are not written into the Constitution, *Griswold* was a milestone. It demonstrated that the Court was willing to go beyond the strict adherence to the language of the Constitution to protect those rights.

### RIGHT OF PRIVACY FOR UNMARRIED CITIZENS

About the time *Griswold* was being decided, another battle was being mounted. This time, it concerned the rights of unmarried citizens to use birth control. The one-man army was William R. Baird, a former medical student who, like Margaret Sanger, discovered his life's mission after watching a young woman die from a botched abortion. Baird, however, was never part of the reproductive rights movement. In fact, he found Planned Parenthood to be a "middle-class monopoly." With equal disdain, former Planned Parenthood president Loraine Campbell called him a "thorn in our flesh for years," though she admitted that in the long run he "did more good than harm."[2]

In May 1965, one month before the *Griswold* decision was announced, Baird staged one of his first acts of civil disobedience: handing out contraceptives in a small New York town where it was illegal to distribute birth control devices without a license. His plan to bring attention to that New York law ultimately backfired; he was arrested but not prosecuted. The only repercussion of the arrest was his dismissal from employment with a pharmaceutical company.

Two years later, Baird set out to test a Massachusetts law that permitted only doctors to prescribe means of birth control and only to married people. At a speaking engagement at Boston University, before a crowd of about 2,000, Baird called volunteers from the audience to hand out packages of contraceptive foam. At the same time, he urged the police officers who were stationed about the hall to arrest him so that he could take his case to court. The police obliged. Baird was arrested and taken to the police station. He pleaded not guilty and was released on bail of $100.

After a short nonjury trial in Massachusetts Superior Court, Baird was convicted of violating the statute. His appeal failed to persuade the highest Massachusetts court that the statute was unconstitutional. It affirmed his conviction by a vote of four to three and sentenced him to three months in prison.

Luckily for Baird, the U.S. Supreme Court voted to hear his appeal of the conviction. An earlier appeal filed by Baird had been rejected and, as a result, he had served thirty-five days in the Charles Street Jail in Boston. It is interesting to note that Baird's crime was distributing products that were on the shelves in most drugstores. It was also at about this time, in 1970, that the federal Comstock laws were finally redrafted to remove birth control materials from the obscene materials category.

In March 1972, six justices of the Supreme Court affirmed a decision by the federal First Circuit Court of Appeals that had voided the Massachusetts statute. Justice William J. Brennan, Jr., drafted the majority opinion. It was, in some ways, a difficult decision to understand. The *Griswold* decision, which first established the right to use contraception, was connected explicitly to "the sacred precincts of *marital* bedrooms."[3] Now, Justice Brennan was extending a right that had its roots in marriage to unmarried people. "The rights must be the same for the unmarried and the married alike," he wrote in *Eisenstadt v. Baird*.[4] He explained it this way:

> *It is true that in* Griswold *the right of privacy in question inhered in the marital relationship. Yet the marital couple is not an independent entity with a mind and heart of its own, but an association of two individuals each with a separate intellectual and emotional makeup. If the right of privacy means anything, it is the right of the* individual, *married or single, to be free from unwarranted governmental intrusion into matters so fundamentally affecting a person as the decision whether to bear or beget a child.*[5]

The decision was an important one, probably more for what it suggested than for what it said outright. In 1972, the movement to legalize abortion was active and state antiabortion laws were being challenged in the courts. However, the Supreme Court had not yet issued an opinion on the legality of abortion. In this context, Justice Brennan's words had special significance. Supporters of legalized abortion could not help but feel hopeful for an eventual victory when they read his statement that the "right of privacy . . . is the right of the *individual* . . . to be free from . . . governmental intrusion into . . . the decision whether to bear or beget a child."

### ROE v. WADE

Sarah Weddington was closely watching the U.S. Supreme Court in 1972 when *Eisenstadt* was decided. For the previous three years, she had been representing Norma McCorvey, better known as Jane Roe of the famous case *Roe v. Wade*.

In 1969, just two years out of law school, Weddington was asked by a women's group in Austin, Texas, to file a test case to challenge a state statute prohibiting abortion. Setting up the case was tough, but she accepted. They needed a plaintiff who was pregnant and wanted an abortion when the case was filed. If the plaintiff got an illegal abortion or delivered a child before filing the case, a court might find that because the issue had already been resolved, there was no need for a decision.

Norma McCorvey was in her early twenties and pregnant for the third time when she met Weddington. McCorvey wanted an abortion but had not found services she could afford. A young woman with a troubled past, McCorvey had stolen money to run away from home at ten, attended reform school until ninth grade, and had her first child at sixteen. After her husband beat her, she returned

*Sarah Weddington, the attorney who argued before the Supreme Court in the controversial* Roe v. Wade *case*

to her mother's house with her young daughter. When it was clear to Norma's mother that Norma was bisexual, she moved away with Norma's daughter and eventually got custody. Norma worked in a variety of odd jobs, abused alcohol and drugs, and, at nineteen, had a second child, whom she gave up for adoption.

Weddington was introduced to McCorvey through an adoption attorney and Linda Coffee, an attorney working with Weddington. The pregnant Norma McCorvey hoped that she would be able to get the abortion that she wanted and raised the issue with the two attorneys. Perhaps because they needed a pregnant plaintiff and perhaps because McCorvey was already four months along in her pregnancy, Sarah Weddington did not help her obtain an abortion, a fact that still angers Norma McCorvey. In a 1994 interview, she explained her anger: "Sarah sat right across the table from me at Columbo's pizza parlor, and I didn't know until two years ago that she had had an abortion herself. When I told her then how desperately I needed one, she could have told me where to go for it. But she wouldn't because she needed me to be pregnant for her case. . . . It was one of the most hideous times of my life."[6]

The case was initiated when Linda Coffee filed a complaint in the name of Jane Roe against Henry Wade, the Dallas County district attorney, on March 3, 1970. In it she asserted that the Texas statute denied Jane Roe the "right to safe and adequate medical advice pertaining to the decision of whether to carry a given pregnancy to term" and denied all women the "right to privacy in the physician-patient relationship."[7]

*Roe v. Wade* progressed through the courts. A hearing was held before a three-judge panel of the

U.S. district court in Dallas. After the hearing, the judges reached a decision in less than five minutes. "It was actually an easy case for us," recalled Irving Goldberg, one of the judges on the panel. "The statute we had before us was clearly bad. It made criminal almost any type of abortion by anyone. . . . You cannot tell me that a woman who gets pregnant due to rape cannot have the burden removed from her body."[8] The court declared the Texas statute unconstitutional in a short opinion that quoted from Arthur J. Goldberg's concurrence in *Griswold*. District Attorney Henry Wade vowed to appeal the case to the U.S. Supreme Court. In May 1971, the Supreme Court announced that it would hear arguments in *Roe* in the fall of that year.

The oral argument was scheduled for December 13. In her argument, Sarah Weddington emphasized the effect pregnancy had on a woman's life.

*A pregnancy to a woman is perhaps one of the most determinative aspects of her life. It disrupts her education. It disrupts her employment. And it often disrupts her family life. . . . Because of the impact on women, this certainly . . . is a matter which is of such fundamental and basic concern to the woman involved that she should be allowed to make the choice as to whether to continue or terminate her pregnancy.*

She further argued that the Constitution "as I see it, gives protection to people after birth."[9]

Jay Floyd, the attorney for the state of Texas, argued that there was no precedent for the right to have total control over one's body and cited the state's outlawing of drugs and adultery as examples of when the state dictated an individual's actions involving his body. He further asserted that "there is life from the moment of impregnation," and closed by stating that the matter was best resolved in the Texas legislature.[10]

After much negotiation, drafting, and redrafting, the Court issued its decision in *Roe* on January 22, 1973. Harry A. Blackmun authored the fifty-one-page opinion for the seven-to-two majority. The foundation for the decision was the right of privacy that had been established in *Griswold* and expanded in *Eisenstadt*.

> *The Constitution does not explicitly mention any right of privacy. In a line of decisions, however . . . the Court has recognized that a right of personal privacy, or a guarantee of certain areas or zones of privacy, does exist under the Constitution. . . .*
>
> *This right of privacy . . . is broad enough to encompass a woman's decision whether or not to terminate her pregnancy.[11]*

Blackmun concluded that "the word 'person,' as used in the Fourteenth Amendment, does not include the unborn." As to the scope of the right of privacy, Blackmun declared that women did not have an "absolute" right, and he attempted to define the limits on the right to privacy in the abortion context. "The right of privacy . . . is broad enough to cover the abortion decision; and the right, nonetheless, is not absolute and is subject to some limitations; and that at some point the state interests as to protection of health, medical standards, and prenatal life, become dominant. We agree with this approach."[12]

The opinion provided a timetable for women

*Norma McCorvey, or Jane Roe of* Roe v. Wade, *is surrounded by reporters in front of the Capitol during a 1989 prochoice rally; she has since declared herself an antiabortion supporter.*

seeking abortions. Dividing pregnancy into three trimesters, Blackmun devised a formula for determining when the state could regulate or proscribe abortion entirely. In the first trimester (approximately three months), the decision to have an abortion is up to the woman and her doctor. In the second trimester, states could pass regulations restricting abortion procedures in ways that protected the mother's health. In the third trimester, because the fetus could potentially live outside the womb, states could prohibit abortion unless the mother's health or life were at stake.

Across the nation, reactions to the decision by the public were and continue to be intense. Supporters of women's reproductive freedom hailed the case as a landmark. The nation's mainstream media, for the most part, echoed this sentiment, calling the decision "wise and sound," "sensible," and "persuasive." Opponents of abortion, such as the Roman Catholic archbishop Terence Cardinal Cooke, denounced the opinion as "shocking and horrifying."[13]

As for Norma McCorvey, she first learned of the decision when she read about it in the newspaper. Only then did she admit to anyone, including the woman she was living with, that she was Jane Roe. In an ironic twist in the *Roe v. Wade* story, Norma McCorvey has recently declared her support for the antiabortion movement.

### BOWERS v. HARDWICK

The next test for *Griswold's* right of privacy would, like the abortion issue, be around an issue that was highly controversial. How far would *Griswold* stretch? With both *Eisenstadt* and *Roe*, the Court had been willing to expand the right of privacy to include the personal choices individuals must make around childbearing and family planning. Was there also a right that protected, simply, physical intimacy inside the home?

The Supreme Court answered that question with a flat no in 1986 when it decided the case of *Bowers v. Hardwick*. Michael Hardwick was a twenty-eight-year-old gay man living in Atlanta, Georgia. In 1982, he was given a ticket for drinking in public when he left a bar carrying a beer. Although Hardwick paid his fine, a few weeks later a police officer arrived at Hardwick's home with a warrant for his arrest for nonappearance in court. A guest let him into Hardwick's bedroom, where he saw Hardwick engaging in oral sex with another man. The officer proceeded to arrest Hardwick for sodomy. Unsure about securing a conviction given the circumstances of the arrest, the prosecutor decided not to press the sodomy charge.

However, Michael Hardwick was angered by the experience and he decided to question the constitutionality of the statute. He filed a declaratory judgment case naming Georgia's attorney general, Michael Bowers, as the defendant. His goal was a ruling that sexual conduct between consenting adults was protected by the right of privacy.

Justice Byron R. White drafted the five-to-four majority opinion that was issued on June 30, 1986. In reaching its decision, the U.S. Supreme Court focused on the plaintiff's homosexuality, not on the broader principle of a constitutional right to conduct intimate relationships in the privacy of one's own home. According to the majority of the Court, the issue in *Bowers* was "whether the Federal Constitution confers a fundamental right upon homosexuals to engage in sodomy." The answer was no. Neither *Griswold*, nor *Eisenstadt*, nor *Roe* an-

*Michael Hardwick was the defendant in the
Georgia sodomy case that went before the Supreme
Court in 1986 and tested the limits of right of
privacy as outlined in* Griswold.

nounced rights that resembled in any way "the
claimed constitutional right of homosexuals to engage in sodomy. . . . No connection between family,
marriage, or procreation on the one hand and homosexual activity on the other has been demonstrated."[14]

A forceful dissent was filed by Justice Harry A.
Blackmun and joined by Justices William J. Brennan, Jr., Thurgood Marshall, and John Paul
Stevens. Blackmun decried the way the majority
had cast the issue in the case. "This case is about

'the most comprehensive of rights and the right most valued by civilized men,' namely 'the right to be let alone,' " he wrote. Because the statute applied to heterosexuals as well as homosexuals, Blackmun saw the majority's focus on Hardwick's sexual preference as intolerant of homosexual lifestyles and as intrusive of all citizens' rights to pursue intimate relationships without government proscription. "Depriving individuals of the right to choose for themselves how to conduct their intimate relationships poses a far greater threat to the values most deeply rooted in our Nation's history than tolerance of nonconformity could ever do."[15]

## WEBSTER v. REPRODUCTIVE HEALTH SERVICES

After *Bowers*, the next cases establishing the boundaries of the right of privacy would again concern abortion. In 1989, the Court had an opportunity to reconsider its decision legalizing abortion in *Roe v. Wade* when it voted to hear *Webster v. Reproductive Health Services*. The state of Missouri had adopted several regulations that restricted abortion, and thus far they had not held up to court challenge. Missouri's attorney general, William L. Webster, submitted a brief that attacked *Roe* on all fronts and asserted that the state's interest in protecting life at all stages in pregnancy was greater than the right of privacy.

The Court was as divided on the issues raised in *Webster* as the rest of the nation was on the issue of abortion. In a nationwide poll taken at the time, only slightly more than 50 percent of those asked said that they supported the *Roe* decision. Ultimately, the Court declined to overrule *Roe*, but it did "modify and narrow" it by allowing provisions of the Missouri law that significantly restricted access to abortion. The decision is a patchwork of concurrences and dissents. Even the majority opinion is broken into sections in which the justices pick and choose the parts they agree to support. Dissenting opinions filed by Justices Stevens and Blackmun, joined by Marshall and Brennan, were poignant. Justice Blackmun expressed the sentiment that abortion was endangered and predicted eventual reversal of *Roe* when he called the decision "ominous" and observed that for abortion rights "a chill wind blows."[16]

After *Webster*, other cases continued to push for greater restrictions on access to abortion, and, thus, on the right of privacy. For instance, the Court upheld state laws requiring teenagers to notify one or both parents before receiving an abortion and prohibiting federally funded clinics from counseling patients about abortion. (President Clinton later revoked that ban on the twentieth anniversary of *Roe v. Wade.*)

### PLANNED PARENTHOOD v. CASEY

Proponents of a woman's right to choose feared for the health of *Roe.* Even if it were not explicitly overturned, it seemed not unlikely that it would be rendered null as states were allowed to enact greater and tighter restrictions on abortion. Then, the Court agreed to hear argument in *Planned Parenthood of Southeastern Pennsylvania v. Casey.* *Casey* required the Court to determine whether Pennsylvania's 1989 Abortion Control Act was constitutional. The act severely restricted abortion by requiring, among other things, that the woman's husband be notified before an abortion is performed and that the woman receive counseling and wait twenty-four hours before having an abortion performed. The case also provided the highly conservative Court with the opportunity to review *Roe* once again. After *Webster* and in light of the previous stances the justices had taken on the abortion issue, few observers expected *Roe* to survive in any recognizable form.

It was, then, a great surprise when, on June 29, 1992, Justices Sandra Day O'Connor, Anthony M. Kennedy, and David H. Souter read from the opinion that they had coauthored and that unequivocally announced *Roe* was alive and well. The opinion described the three parts of *Roe* that it reaffirmed. The first was "the right of the woman to choose to have an abortion before viability and to obtain it without undue interference from the State." Second was "the State's power to restrict abortions after fetal viability, if the law contains exceptions for pregnancies which endanger a woman's life or health." Finally, the opinion protected the "principle that the State has legitimate interests from the outset of the pregnancy in protecting the health of the woman and the life of the fetus that may become a child."

The decision also reaffirmed *Griswold*, acknowledging that "in some critical respects the abortion decision is of the same character as the decision to use contraception," and stating that "We have no doubt as to the correctness of those decisions. As such, *Griswold* was one of the cases that support the reasoning in *Roe* relating to the woman's liberty."

*Planned Parenthood of Southeastern Pennsylvania v. Casey* also allowed states to adopt regulations that ensure that the woman's choice to have an abortion "is thoughtful and informed." For, although the case affirmed *Roe*'s constitutional analysis that gave women the right to choose to have an abortion, the Court was clear that that right was "not so unlimited . . . that from the outset the State cannot show its concern for the life of the unborn."[17]

## A HEATED ISSUE

Despite the Court's attempt in *Casey* to find a workable compromise on the abortion issue, the struggle between prochoice and antiabortion forces continues to rage. Some antiabortion strategies have included staging political rallies, picketing abortion clinics, and making public the names of doctors who perform abortions.

At times, the struggle has turned violent. On December 31, 1994, John Salvi III shot and killed two receptionists and wounded several other employees at two family-planning clinics in Massachusetts. Only months earlier, in July 1994, Paul Hill, former minister and member of Defensive Action, which advocates the use of violence to end abortion, gunned down a doctor on his way to work at an abortion clinic in Pensacola, Florida. The doctor's bodyguard was also killed. More than a year earlier, in March 1993, Michael Griffin shot dead another doctor outside another clinic in Pensacola.

Such actions do not represent the mainstream opponents of abortion. Operation Rescue and the Catholic Church have denounced such shootings categorically. "The pro-life movement has no room for violence or vigilantism. There are no qualifiers," said one of the leaders of Operation Rescue. The shootings do, however, show the feeling of desperation brewing in some of the more radical groups. Don Treshman, director of the antiabortion group Rescue America, responded to the shootings at the Massachusetts clinics: "We're in a war. The only thing is that until recently the casualties have only been on one side. There are 30 million dead babies

*Activists from both sides of the abortion issue
face off in front of the Supreme Court. The matter
is far from resolved.*

and only five people on the other side, so it's really nothing to get all excited about."[18]

The controversy that unfolded in *Griswold v. Connecticut* embodies the continuing tension that exists between individual liberties, such as the right to use birth control or to have an abortion, and the state's authority, which includes restricting or prohibiting certain acts or practices through laws and regulations. *Griswold* resolved that tension as it relates to birth control. But in identifying a right of privacy, the Supreme Court has opened the door to a host of other questions. What does the right of privacy encompass? How far does it reach? The right of privacy that emerged in *Griswold v. Connecticut* is probably secure. However, the decision that rests upon it—the decision to legalize abortion—is one of the most controversial issues of our time. And on that issue, the U.S. Supreme Court will surely have more to say.

# SOURCE NOTES

## CHAPTER 1

1. Fred W. Friendly and Martha J. H. Elliot, *The Constitution: That Delicate Balance* (New York: Random House, 1984), 196.

2. Gereon Zimmerman, "Contraception and Commotion in Connecticut," *Look*, January 30, 1962, 80.

3. Ibid.

4. David J. Garrow, *Liberty and Sexuality: The Right to Privacy and the Making of Roe v. Wade* (New York: Macmillan, 1994), 16.

5. Zimmerman, 80–81.

6. *New York Times*, September 19, 1987, 10.

7. *Newsweek*, June 21, 1965, 60.

8. 367 U.S. 497, 508 (1961).

## CHAPTER 2

1. C. Thomas Dienes, *Law, Politics and Birth Control* (Urbana: University of Illinois Press, 1972), 32.

2. Heywood Broun and Margaret Leech, *Anthony*

*Comstock: Roundsman of the Lord and Birth Control* (New York: Albert and Charles Boni, 1927), 55–56.

3. Eva R. Rubin, ed., *The Abortion Controversy: A Documentary History* (Westport, Conn.: Greenwood Press, 1994), 27.

4. Garrow, 16.

5. David M. Kennedy, *Birth Control in America: The Career of Margaret Sanger* (New Haven, Conn.: Yale University Press, 1970), 2.

6. Ibid., 16–17.

7. Broun and Leech, 11.

8. Ellen Chesler, *Woman of Valor: Margaret Sanger and the Birth Control Movement in America* (New York: Simon and Schuster, 1992), 156–158.

9. Ibid., 225.

10. Garrow, 17.

11. Ibid., 19.

12. Ibid., 21.

13. Ibid.

14. Ibid., 23.

15. Ibid.

16. Chesler, 371–372, and Kennedy, 241.

17. *United States v. One Package*, 86 F.2d 737, 739 (2d Cir. 1936).

18. Garrow, 42.

### CHAPTER 3

1. Garrow, 5.

2. Ibid., 7–8.

3. Ibid., 67–68.

4. Ibid., 69.

5. Friendly and Elliot, 193.

6. Garrow, 75.

7. Ibid., 82.

8. Ibid., 83.

9. Ibid., 92–93.

10. Ibid., 94.
11. *Tileston v. Ullman*, 129 Conn. at 86, 96, 26 A.2d 582, 588 (1942).

**CHAPTER 4**
1. Friendly and Elliot, 189.
2. Ibid.
3. Garrow, 134.
4. Ibid.
5. Ibid., 136–137.
6. Ibid., 139.
7. Catherine Roraback, "*Griswold v. Connecticut*: A Brief Case History," 16 *Ohio Northern Law Review* 395 (1989): 397.
8. Friendly and Elliot, 190.
9. Roraback, 397.
10. Garrow, 142.
11. Ibid., 155–156.
12. Ibid., 157–158.
13. Roraback, 399.
14. Garrow, 167–168.
15. Ibid., 171.
16. Ibid., 174.
17. Ibid., 179–180.
18. Ibid., 180.
19. *Poe v. Ullman*, 367 U.S. 497, 508 (1961).
20. Ibid., at 509.
21. Ibid., at 513.
22. Ibid., at 522–555.

**CHAPTER 5**
1. Garrow, 196.
2. Ibid.
3. Zimmerman, 83a.
4. Garrow, 201.
5. Ibid.
6. Ibid., 209.

7. Ibid., 209–210.
8. Ibid., 215.
9. Ibid., 211.
10. Ibid., 212.
11. Ibid., 217.
12. Ibid., 218.
13. Ibid., 222–223.

## CHAPTER 6

1. Garrow, 233.
2. Ibid., 238.
3. Ibid., 239.
4. Ibid., 240.
5. Ibid., 241.
6. *Griswold v. Connecticut*, 381 U.S. at 482.
7. Ibid., at 484–485.
8. Ibid., at 483–484.
9. Ibid., at 485–486.
10. Ibid., at 495–496.
11. Ibid., at 500.
12. Ibid., at 508–510.
13. Ibid., at 527.
14. *New York Times*, June 9, 1965, 46.
15. Garrow, 256.
16. Ibid., 258.

## CHAPTER 7

1. Garrow, 669–671.
2. Ibid., 322–323.
3. *Griswold v. Connecticut*, 381 U.S. at 485.
4. *Eisenstadt v. Baird*, 405 U.S. 438, 453 (1972).
5. Ibid.
6. *New York Times,* July 28, 1994, B4.
7. Garrow, 406.
8. Ibid., 451.
9. Friendly and Elliot, 205.
10. Ibid.

11. *Roe v. Wade*, 410 U.S. 113, 152–153 (1973).
12. Ibid., at 155.
13. Garrow, 605–606.
14. *Bowers v. Hardwick*, 478 U.S. 186, 190–191 (1986).
15. Ibid., at 199.
16. *Webster v. Reproductive Health Services*, 488 U.S. 1003 (1989).
17. Ibid., at 488.
18. *New York Times*, January 1, 1995.

# FOR FURTHER READING

By far, the most comprehensive account of *Griswold v. Connecticut* is David Garrow's *Liberty and Sexuality: The Right to Privacy and the Making of Roe v. Wade* (New York: Macmillan, 1994). Garrow's book chronicles the events that preceded the decision and illustrates the impact *Griswold* had on American legal history, including how abortion rights grew out of *Griswold*'s right of privacy. A lighter treatment of the case and the players is provided in Fred Friendly and Martha J. H. Elliot's collection of essays about cases that interpret the U.S. Constitution, *The Constitution: That Delicate Balance* (New York: Random House, 1984). In an article in *Look* magazine (January 30, 1962), "Contraception and Commotion in Connecticut," Gereon Zimmerman provides a journalist's perspective on the events that sparked the case. This article is particularly valuable for its look at the people behind the case.

Those wishing to learn more about Margaret Sanger should read Ellen Chesler's excellent biography, *Woman of Valor: Margaret Sanger and the Birth Control Movement in America* (New York: Simon and Schuster, 1992). David M. Kennedy's *Birth Control in America: The Career of Margaret Sanger* (New Haven, Conn.: Yale University Press, 1970) is also informative. A colorful, if somewhat dated, portrait of Anthony Comstock can be found in Heywood Broun and Margaret Leech's *Anthony Comstock: Roundsman of the Lord and Birth Control* (New York: Albert and Charles Boni, 1927). C. Thomas Dienes's *Law, Politics and Birth Control* (Urbana: University of Illinois Press, 1972) examines the controversy in detail. Linda Gordon's *Woman's Body: Woman's Right* (New York: Penguin, rev. ed., 1990) provides an interesting historical look at birth control that helps illustrate the source of the debate.

There are several books by William O. Douglas, the U.S. Supreme Court justice who authored the *Griswold* opinion. *The Court Years, 1939–1975: The Autobiography of William O. Douglas* (New York: Random House, 1980) provides much insight into Douglas's thinking.

*Griswold* is noteworthy largely because it provided the foundation on which the right to an abortion rests. Books on the abortion controversy abound. Sarah Weddington's *A Question of Choice* (New York: Putnam, 1992) and Norma McCorvey's *I Am Roe: My Life, Roe v. Wade, and Freedom of Choice* (New York: HarperCollins, 1994) are recent works by the lawyer and plaintiff in the seminal *Roe v. Wade*.

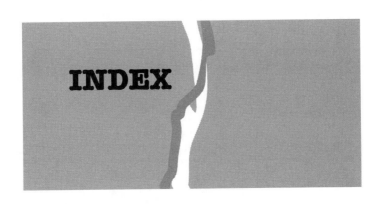

# INDEX

## ABOUT THE AUTHOR

**SUSAN C. WAWROSE**, a graduate of Wellesley College and Northeastern University School of Law, currently works as an attorney. Ms. Wawrose lives in Oxford, Ohio, with her husband and son Jeremiah. This is her first book for Franklin Watts.